D1521153

Access to Inequality

Access to Inequality

Reconsidering Class, Knowledge, and Capital in Higher Education

Amy E. Stich

LEXINGTON BOOKS
Lanham • Boulder • New York • Toronto • Plymouth, UK

Published by Lexington Books
A wholly owned subsidiary of The Rowman & Littlefield Publishing Group, Inc.
4501 Forbes Boulevard, Suite 200, Lanham, Maryland 20706
www.rowman.com

10 Thornbury Road, Plymouth PL6 7PP, United Kingdom

British Library Cataloguing in Publication Information Available

Library of Congress Cataloging-in-Publication Data

Stich, Amy E., 1980-
Access to inequality : reconsidering class, knowledge, and capital in higher education / Amy E. Stich.
p. cm.
Includes bibliographical references and index.
ISBN 978-0-7391-6932-2 (cloth : alk. paper) -- ISBN 978-0-7391-6933-9 (electronic)
1. Education, Higher--Social aspects--United States. 2. Education, Higher--Economic aspects--United States. 3. Educational equalization--United States. I. Title.
LC191.94.S75 2012
306.43'2--dc23

2012025370

Printed in the United States of America

For my mother, Linda A. Wood, and my father, Donald F. Stich, who labored their lives, creative minds at rest, with sacrifice, without complaint, for me.
This labor, my dear parents, is for you.

Table of Contents

Acknowledgments   ix

1   The Democratization of American Higher Education   1

2   Class, Knowledge, and Capital in Interrelated Contexts   13

3   Reputational *Affects:* Inside a Working Class College   29

4   *Class*ifying Knowledge by Hand, by Head   49

5   Elite Knowledge within a Non-Elite Context: Language, Literacy, and "Intertextual Habituality"   69

6   Re-Conceiving Democratization   105

Appendix   117

References   123

Index   131

About the Author   135

Acknowledgments

Because this book is based upon my dissertation research, I extend my deepest gratitude to the members of my dissertation committee, Professors Gregory Dimitriadis, Lois Weis, and Julia Colyar, all of whom have become the best kind of mentors and friends, continuing to deepen my understanding of the social world, and inspire my readerly and writerly mind. In this regard, I also wish to thank Dr. Michael Farrell for his critical insight as a fourth reader on the original version of my dissertation. Additionally, I wish to extend my gratitude to the graduate students (both former and current) in the Graduate School of Education at the University at Buffalo—a community of young scholars who have provided me with perspective and support throughout this process. In particular, I would like to thank my dear friend and colleague, Kristin Cipollone. In addition to those already mentioned, there are countless individuals who have sustained their early influence and support. Among them, I would like to thank two very special women, Drs. Kelly Ahuna and Christine Gray-Tinnesz.

I am, of course, indebted to my family for their unconditional love, patience, support, and encouragement throughout the writing of my first book. They are: Don Stich and Linda Wood, Carolyn Hendrix, April Stich, Amanda Hastings, and Jennifer VanRysdam; and to my Canadian family, Ron, Dianne, and Michael Boyko. And, most of all, I am grateful to my partner, Robin Boyko, for sharing a life with me and the intimate history from which these words were born. In an uncharacteristic moment of religious proclamation, thank God for you.

I also extend my gratitude to the students, teachers, and administrators of McKinley College and the staff of the McKinley Museum of Art who offered their time and opened their lives to me with generosity, and with incredible moments of insight. Finally, I would like to thank Jana Hodges-Kluck and Lexington Books for seeing this through to publication.

. . . *the goal of sociology is to uncover the most deeply buried structures of the different social worlds that make up the social universe, as well as the 'mechanisms' that tend to ensure their reproduction or transformation.*
—*Pierre Bourdieu, 1998, The State Nobility: Elite schools in the field of power*

Chapter One

The Democratization of American Higher Education

Driving down a sinuous stretch of highway, my eyes lift towards a towering billboard perched over the earthen periphery of McKinley College.[1] The ground wraps around the College creating an intense, speed-driven edge to its northern-most border beneath the billboard's enormous black font that reads, "From Homeless to Harvard"—a message from the non-profit organization, *Foundation for a Better Life*. On this particular day, though I have driven along this highway on countless trips to McKinley, I notice these words and feel their meritocratic message, poised by the power of Liz Murray's personal ambition. A larger-than-life image of Liz holding a Psychology textbook sitting within a Harvard lecture hall is positioned next to the bold font that defines her success. Liz's story inspires and provokes the circulation of ambition among youth across America, and in this case, it touches down upon the youth of the beleaguered economy of Arkive, New York, wherein this research takes place. Liz's transition to Harvard is a message to drivers and passersby—it is a message of hope to this economically distressed community and the promise of success captured by individual ambition and knuckle-bearing, honest, hard work. Though meant to inspire, this message is far from neutral situated inside of a highly stratified system of education in which "schools and colleges are the vessels of our meritocratic aspirations" (Soares, 2007). And though perhaps without intention, it enables meritocratic ideology to circulate throughout Arkive's urban air, touching upon commuting students on their way to class at McKinley College—"the Harvard on the lake," as an aged professor used to refer to the school in his thick German accent. Years ago, as an undergraduate student at McKinley, I knew, along with my peers, that this comparison was merely a breath of condescension. Indeed, McKinley is not Harvard, and Liz is not *all* or even *most* disadvantaged youth. She is, indeed, the exception.

Though a comparatively small percentage of students from economically disadvantaged backgrounds do enroll in and graduate from four-year American universities, including elite institutions such as Harvard (Bowen & Bok, 2000), these students are few among the majority of their higher-income peers. Statistics that track the percentages of low-income students' attendance at the most elite institutions make the argument for meritocracy all the more problematic and all the more transparent. In fact, as the American system of higher education continues to experience the effects of economic, social, and political shift causing an increase in selectivity and competition across tiers, the percentage of low-income student enrollment to 4-year institutions becomes increasingly small (Bowen, Chingos, & McPherson, 2009). Of course, these educational disparities lead to other forms of inequality (e.g., greater lifetime earnings).

During the 2008-2009 school year when this research was conducted, McKinley was designated as a categorically less-selective, tier 3,[2] public institution, at the opposite end of Harvard's tier 1, historically elite position within the solidly built hierarchy of higher education. Students who have experienced homelessness or disadvantage, like Liz, do not typically go to Harvard; in fact, they do not typically attend the less-selective McKinley College nor do they typically attend college at all,[3] which is why Liz's story is so compelling and acquires a 45-foot backdrop to our early morning commute. This is the kind of mobility that demands our attention.

As a backdrop and visual to the invisible tension between expressions of the human condition (e.g., ambition) and the structural obstacles that interfere with the movement of many towards desired educational goals, this billboard introduces us to the rusted edge of a rust-belt landscape wherein struggle is all around. Situated on the perimeter of McKinley College, on the edge of a highway system that contributes to the geographic and residential segregation of the Black urban poor from the rest of the population of Arkive (Kraus, 2004), Liz's story reminds us that the path from *Homeless to Harvard* is billboard-worthy within an increasingly competitive system with increasingly demanding admissions requirements (Stevens, 2008). Liz's story also reminds us that elite institutions of higher education occupy positions within the system that enable others to remain situated at the opposite end. Though sharing a common institutional purpose, relationally produced lines of distinction are thickly displayed by socially constructed reputations and categorizations (e.g., institutional rankings), all of which position the two schools at opposite ends of a vertically drawn space. Within this space, it is perhaps more natural to look "up" or to "climb" than to "fall" back or to look "down" toward institutions of lesser distinction. In other words, this powerful image brings Harvard to McKinley, but it does not bring McKinley to Harvard.

But, what might happen if we did bring McKinley to Harvard, if only as an imagined reality? What might happen if we repositioned this signage on the perimeter of Harvard's campus and reworked its text to read "From Homeless to McKinley"? Though the message is not about Harvard, but of one woman's personal ambition, it does tell us something about the potency and unintended consequence of socially embedded messages. When we replace Harvard with McKinley, or rather, the "elite" with the "non-elite," what happens to the image, the message, and the ways in which both are received? By replacing the elite institution with the image of a tier-3, less selective institution, do we reduce the power of the message? Do Liz's ambitions wane under the new weight of an altered institutional reputation? Though the message may continue to hold its inherent meaning, does it lose its dramatic edge as the backdrop to ambition? In this textual flip, we not only lose the engaging sound of alliteration, but, arguably, we also lose a great deal of effect and perhaps good sense in the absence of Harvard—the iconic, elite institution. Indeed, the Harvard communicated by the billboard is a socially constructed ideal. It is the weight of prestige and the power of rank. To summon René Magritte,[4] it is not the *real* institution. If we pull back the veneer of an idealized Harvard, replace it with the relatively unknown McKinley College, and relocate this message to Harvard's campus perimeter, it would seem that we are left with an illogical reversal. But what makes this message lose its power, logic and sense?

Images are reflective surfaces. They carry the potency of popular discourse and dispel these messages back onto viewers who then return them to the social space from which they originated. Like all images, the billboard's power lies in the ways it penetrates context and in the ways context penetrates the billboard so that it becomes infused with meaning and social consequence, both of which so often go unnoticed. If meaning and social consequence of an image are dependent upon where and by whom they are received, then shifting the context alone alters a great deal (both the context of the message, the iconic Harvard University, and the context wherein it is received, McKinley College). As Pierre Bourdieu asserts: "Meaning and social efficacy of a given message is determined only within a given field" (Bourdieu & Wacquant, 1992, p.149). Bourdieu's notion of field, which will be referred to and relied upon heavily throughout this book, allows for an understanding of the relationships within and among institutions. Considering McKinley's position within the field of higher education relative to Harvard's causes little pause; it is, simply, of lower rank, status, and value. The established hierarchy provides the direction from an acceptable low to the invaluable high and we struggle to imagine a rearrangement of this "natural" order. In this way, the logic of the field of power is unidirectional, moving only towards the top—a cue to the collective unconscious, one that is involuntary and would jerk, vomit, twist, and turn on itself before turning toward the perceived bottom. To be sure, the products, knowledge, and culture of the elite are always "made accessible" to the non-elite. The reversal, however, remains inconceivable. But imagining a billboard that reads "From Homeless to McKinley" is exactly what this book aims to do. Envisioning this very simple contextual flip requires that our thinking dislodge itself from the very difficult limitations presented by a very resistant field of power, one that includes the academic space within which we work.

In this book, not unlike the billboard, McKinley College is also a reflective surface. As an institution, it resounds with the systemic discourse of higher education. Although McKinley College is but one institution among thousands in the immense and varying American system of higher education, this research resonates beyond its immediate, singular location. McKinley, though a unique case discussed at a particular time, becomes at once, as Bourdieu describes of the French academic universe, both particular and general. A goal of Bourdieu's analysis of the French academy is "to show that the opposition between the universal and the unique, between nomothetic analysis and idiographic description, is a false antimony" (Bourdieu & Wacquant, 1992, p. 75). McKinley, then, like Bourdieu's case of the French academy, becomes a "particular case of the possible" (p.75) where we find evidence of "the same oppositions, in particular, that between academic capital linked to power of the instruments of reproduction and intellectual capital linked to scientific renown" (Bourdieu & Wacquant, 1992, pp. 75-76). As a systemic, relational critique, McKinley College becomes more than an examined singular, unique site, but one that is anchored within the system of education—part of the arbitrary, seemingly natural order of things. Using a relational, field-level perspective allows us to see McKinley College as a particular institution with unique qualities, but also as an institution that, despite its uniqueness, reflects a "particular case of the possible" (p. 75) within the field of higher education (one that is now global in scope). In other words, as a product of democratization, McKinley exemplifies other tier-2, lower-ranking schools in size, organization, student demographics, and mission, among other more general characteristics (nationally and, in many ways, globally). McKinley, as a particular case, is illustrative of democratization, a more general phenomenon.

The research to follow demonstrates the processual and ideological mechanisms that sort and solidify the seemingly natural structure of social space, which includes the system of higher education as its focus, and as an example of one cross-cutting, intersecting field: the art world, wherein the same process of democratization of elite knowledge has paved a very similar and related recent history. As the product of social process and economic shift, the system of higher education continues to transform and experience tremendous change, but all the while, an idle, fertile foundation is buried deep under the surface of this movement.

SURFACE MOVEMENT: SOCIAL PROCESS AND UNREST

The aftermath of WWII brought significant social and institutional change to an otherwise elite trajectory. During this time, the massification of higher education, particularly in the US, but also within other nations, signaled a move towards efforts to democratize—to make the once exclusionary contexts and knowledge of the elite accessible to a wider public. In the US, for example, university enrollment increased quite significantly with the introduction of the GI Bill (Roksa, Grodsky, Arum, & Gamoran, 2007) and need-based financial aid (Astin & Oseguera, 2004). Structurally, the system met significant change with the invention of the community college and institutions focused specifically on vocational[5] and semi-professional education (Roksa, et al., 2007, p. 165). This expansion, particularly aggressive throughout the 1960s, 70s and 80s, has resulted in more than 4,000 institutions of higher education in the US alone, and significant increases in national college enrollment, as well as an increasingly diverse student population (Trow, 2005). In fact, the number of postsecondary institutions increased by more than 50 percent between the 1950 and 2000 (Mullen, 2010). During this time, the system of higher education moved from one characterized as "elite" to one characterized as "mass," or rather, "from educating less than 15 percent of the college-age cohort to educating between 15 and 50 percent of it" (Berdahl, Altbach, & Gumport, 2011, p. 5). With an increasing number of postsecondary institutions, including more recent growth in for-profit institutions, the American system now enrolls more than 20 million students (US Census Bureau, 2012) as opposed to the 2.3 million in 1950 (Mullen, 2010). Today, "63% of high-school graduates enter postsecondary education, and over one-quarter of the population has a college degree" (Roksa et al., 2007, p. 166).

Further observable movement and change introduced the end of the twentieth and beginning of the twenty-first century, an era marked by a sharp turn toward globalization (Gamoran, 2001, 2008; Piketty & Saez, 2001; Reich, 2007, 2008; Thomas & Bell, 2008). As a complex and dominant contemporary social process, globalization has created greater opportunity and economic development for many, but has also been partially responsible for the growing income gap, one that has slowly squeezed security from the lives of the working and middle class (Reich, 2007). Within the US context, growth in income and wealth gaps between the rich and the poor can be attributed to more recent transformations in the occupational structure of the U.S. economy, prompted by the significant turn toward globalization. The economy has shifted from one that is primarily manufacturing-based to one that is knowledge-based (Brown, Lauder, & Ashton, 2011; Reich, 2007, 2008), accompanied by the proliferation of a neoliberal[6] public discourse. Such transformations have led to rising instability among the middle classes in particular, (Reich, 2007, 2008; Thomas & Bell, 2008) as the government reduces or altogether retracts social and economic supports (e.g., financial aid), and as both blue- and white-collar jobs have become part of a "global auction" (Brown, et al., 2011; Weis, 2011). These changes to the organization of labor have created serious challenges for a large cross-section of our society—positions that were once lucrative certainties upon graduation are now the privileges of a select few. Alterations in the labor market have also led to elevated competition and further organizational change in higher education as institutions compete for the "best students" (as well as faculty and resources) and potential students compete for access to "the best" colleges. For the reasons outlined above, projections for both college enrollment and the number of degrees granted suggest that these patterns will continue between 2011 and 2019 (U.S. Department of Education, 2011).

At the surface level, democratization, expansion, and increasing numbers of students entering higher education from more diverse socioeconomic backgrounds provide a global image of greater access and social progress; however, as the US system of higher education, as well as the systems of other developed nations, appear to operate under a more democratic logic—designed to reduce inequality—institutional and knowledge-based hierarchization prevent real social progress from materializing. As these durable hierarchies pervade higher education, it is argued that the system of higher education today, indeed offering more opportunity, is far from being a vision of equal access, opportunity and outcome. As inequality persists within a system of increasing "access," the *foundation* of social space resists change.

IDLE FOUNDATION: THE STRUCTURE OF INEQUALITIES AT REST

As a result of the expansion in higher education, access to postsecondary institutions has greatly increased for low-income and minority students. Broido (2004) reports that "'minority enrollment will rise both in absolute numbers of students—up about 2 million—and in percentage terms, up from 29.4 percent undergraduate enrollment to 37.2 percent'" (pp. 73-74). These findings are consistent with Murdock and Hoque's (1999) earlier prediction for higher education regarding increases in the diversity of student enrollment. However, the majority of this improved access has occurred largely within 2-year and lower-status 4-year public institutions (Karen, 2002; Roksa et al., 2007). While Bowen and Bok (2000) made an important contribution to the study of race and enrollment in elite education by empirically providing evidence for the positive impact of race-sensitive admissions policies, reminding us of the complexities surrounding race and class, the overwhelming percentage of minority and low-income students continue to enroll in less-selective, non-elite institutions (McDonough & Fann, 2007). Thomas and Perna (2004) conclude: "Virtually all expansion of higher education opportunity has occurred in non-elite institutions . . . Thus, while there now exists greater capacity to accommodate the growing demand for higher education, the new opportunities that this expansion represents are the ones that are quite removed from those provided by the nation's more prestigious (and least accessible) institutions" (p. 45).

It seems then that despite the well-intended, now mature processes of expansion and democratization, the postsecondary system is still charged with high levels of inequality. In fact, as Soares (2007) asserts: "The irony is that education was supposed to be an equal opportunity leveler, but at the top, it has become a mechanism of class stratification" (p. 182). As gaps between groups in the rates of college enrollment and attainment continue to increase along a continuum of institutional rank (enrollment is greatest for low-income students in less prestigious, less-selective colleges and universities where completion and economic returns are lowest, see Perna and Thomas, 2004), recent studies have determined that *where* one goes to college matters as much as, if not more than, *if* one goes to college (Mullen, 2010; Stephan, Rosenbaum & Person, 2009). Few would argue with the notion that there are unequivocal privileges afforded to students attending and graduating from more prestigious, highly selective institutions (Astin, 1993; Astin & Oseguera, 2004) wherein students are provided with knowledge, resources, and opportunities (various forms of social and cultural capital) that enable the accumulation of further privilege. However, these already difficult-to-enter colleges and universities are becoming increasingly so, intensifying competition across all institutional tiers.

In their recent study of 21 state flagship universities, Bowen, Chingos, and McPherson (2009) argue that the elite sector, along with lower-ranking colleges and universities, are becoming more and more selective. According to the authors: "Today, more than 40 percent of the undergraduates at these universities come from families in the top quartile of the income distribution" (p. 17). This increased selectivity has intensified pressure for admittance to elite schools, pushing many privileged students, who would have been admitted in the past, into less-selective institutions (Ellwood & Kane, 2000; Thomas & Bell, 2008; Weis, 2011). Lois Weis (2011) reveals the consequences of this recent trend: "This serves to increasingly drive those who are not middle and/or upper middle class to pursue postsecondary education at relatively low ranking institutions, an empirical turn with grave consequences" (2011, pp.16-17). Increased competition and selectivity across the system of higher education (and across all levels of education) not only makes it exceedingly difficult for minority and low-income students to access elite institutions (Astin & Oseguera, 2004) but this shift also reduces the likelihood of acceptance to second- and third-tier institutions that have recently elevated admissions standards and the cost of tuition, limiting options for many to the 2-year, open admission, community college—also known as the "dumping grounds for poor students" (Mullen, 2010, p. 8). Though increased opportunity alone does indeed demonstrate a certain level of progress, it is not enough, it does not bring us closer to equality, and it is not democratic.

But what differentiates these institutions beyond their positions within such a highly stratified system? How might attending a college or university of lower or higher rank, one that is more or less selective, limit or expand opportunities and shape one's "pathway to prosperity" (Harvard Graduate School of Education, 2011)? What happens within postsecondary institutions to cause such disparity?

While important research has been dedicated to questions of access to this stratified system (who attends what schools and what determines or influences these decisions, see Roksa et al., 2007), less is known about how institutions of higher education (and the people within them) help to maintain and reproduce systemic, class-based stratification. In addition, though scholars have pursued research on institutional differentiation, we know even less about the extent to which knowledge itself becomes differentiated as the result of the highly influential process of democratization. As is argued in the research to follow, though not without methodological limitations (see appendix), differentiation at an institutional level, and at the level of knowledge, maintains and reproduces the unequal structure of higher education as our democratic intentions move farther away from our fixed hierarchical positioning.

THE STUDY

The research presented within this book was born from a single line of inquiry posed in a thought-provoking essay published more than a decade ago by art historian Carol Duncan (1993). In her essay on "Teaching the Rich" Duncan questioned the legitimacy of the democratization of the traditional liberal arts education, challenging assumptions held by educators, administrators, and scholars that "the democratization of elitist liberal arts education is possible" (p. 135). Duncan's intellectual interests and concerns span the length of art history, and in doing so, they take up the space of its institutionalized forms within the university. As an empirical response to Duncan's inquiry, this research seeks to understand the shape and form of elite knowledge, as well as the perceptions of these forms, after they are filtered through the process of democratization.

As part of a liberal arts education, and as an example of elite knowledge within this book, the visual arts occupy an important space within higher education, and also one that is uniquely connected to historical and existing hierarchies of knowledge. As a form of elite knowledge, the visual arts are directly disseminated within two primary contexts: university art history departments and art museums/galleries. Once no more than the exclusionary knowledge of the elite (not unlike higher education itself), the visual arts, through the process of democratization, is now argued to be among the shared, socially-inclusive knowledge of the general public. This phenomenon (democratization) is not one that is singular or removed from the context of other fields, but is interconnected and intricately tied to the field of higher education (Wallach, 2002). The intimate relationship between higher education and the art world not only exemplifies the sharing of knowledge between two seemingly separate and distinct fields (higher education and the art world), but also reveals a great deal about the ways in which general, broad sweeping social processes like democratization structure social space. In using the visual arts as an example of elite knowledge, this year-long qualitative study reveals the beginning of a rather complicated answer to Carol Duncan's original question. As discussed herein, McKinley College's democratized position within the larger system of higher education and its working-class reputation translates into a damaging discursive practice and a corresponding hierarchy of class-based knowledge, providing insight into the mechanisms through which order is maintained within the hierarchical structure of higher education.

Data for this book were collected through 33 in-depth, semi-structured interviews, non-participant observations (including classroom observations), and document analysis. These multiple methods, together and without privileging one over the other, offer a complexity that more closely resembles the social world within which we live. As an instrumental case study[7] (Stake, 2005), McKinley College holds a unique position within social space, but can also be read as one that informs further understanding of similarly located institutions within the system of higher education. McKinley was selected as a primary research site because of this location, rank, and associated art museum (a source of elite knowledge centrally located). The focus of this study is on the process of democratization within the hierarchical field of higher education, but it is also suggestive of cross-cutting fields, like that of the art world, which also highlights the consequences of democratization.

Though this is not a comparative study, it does offer elements of a comparative nature to enhance the power of positionality within the field of higher education. To accomplish these ends, this is done without "glossing over uniqueness or complexities" (Stake, 2005, p. 457) by enlisting materials from purposely selected institutions (e.g., elite liberal arts colleges). The use of these various exploratory methods for qualitative analysis not only offers multiple and dense sources for data, but allows for a richer account of McKinley College. Finally, this study is deeply informed by Pierre Bourdieu's intellectual framework—one that is both methodologically and theoretically bound. Bourdieu's synthesis of theory and practice garnered through a multiple-level reflexivity characterizes and formulates the research to follow.

ORGANIZATION OF CHAPTERS

Taken together, the following chapters illustrate the consequences of democratization as currently conceived. Beginning with an introduction to the theoretical framework informing this research, chapter two introduces the concept of elite knowledge in an interconnected context. This chapter positions McKinley College within a geographic and symbolic field of culture- and knowledge-producing institutions (e.g., institutions of higher education and museums/galleries), all of which help to construct McKinley's institutional working-class identity. This chapter acts as a bridge between the chosen methodology, the theoretical advances made, and the empirical evidence found within this research. To begin, it reviews Bourdieu's relational constructs field (a core concept of Bourdieu's that has received little attention, Bourdieu & Wacquant, 1992; Naidoo, 2004, 2008), habitus, and capital (though in no way is this to be considered a thorough overview of Bourdieu's analytic model) and applies these concepts to the field of higher education. The chapter ends by locating the singular research site (the campus of McKinley College) within its respective and related homologous[8] sub-fields and in further narrowing the focus of study, then describes the immediate contexts of McKinley College the McKinley's Museum of Art (MMA).

Chapter three initiates an empirical response to questions concerning democratization through the socially constructed reputation of McKinley College, its associated community members, and the social-psychological consequences of McKinley's working class reputation as a damaging discursive practice. Further, this chapter demonstrates how participating students, faculty, staff, and administration at McKinley articulate institutional reputation and the reputation of students as related to a stigmatized image of the working class within higher education.

Chapter four seeks to revive the old agenda of the "new" sociology of education — one that challenged the content and form of knowledge itself as contributing to social reproduction (Weis, McCarthy, & Dimitriadis, 2006). The purpose of this particular chapter is to illustrate how the constructions of social realities, in this case, the constructed reality of McKinley's working-class reputation and the reputation of the working class in higher education, shape the structure and content of knowledge, and ultimately, the structure of opportunity. Moving further inside the study of reputation as a conceptual tool to investigate knowledge differentiation, this chapter examines the institutional messages communicated through various college documents and the ways in which these messages are carried through internal representational voices, shaping pedagogy, curricular divisions, student attitudes, and campus culture.

Chapter five interrogates the visual arts as a form of elite knowledge, or rather, academic capital, within the "democratized," "non-elite" discursive space of McKinley College. The chapter begins within the social space of "working-class McKinley," gathering an empirical basis for the interwoven analysis of the relationship between habitus (both that of students and of the institution) and the proliferation of discursive formations surrounding the visual arts (language and literacies). Following this more general vision of the valuation of the arts on campus, the path of analysis moves into the subfield of art history through the study of McKinley's art history program. The trajectory of analysis then advances into the larger field of art history and widens into the relational space of the McKinley Museum of Art, a separate, but related context that is arguably involved in the preservation of elite knowledge and privileged spaces.

The final chapter summarizes the previous four and concludes with a discussion of why our current conception of democratization should be reconceived in order to reverse an overwhelming social debt and provide access to equality.

NOTES

1. In the interest of protecting the identity of participants, all institutions and participants, as well as other unique identifiers, were assigned pseudonyms.

2. Because the formation of institutional reputation sits at the center of this research and rankings play such an important role in the formation of institutional reputation, this research uses the categorization system of the popular *U.S. News and World Report* (USNWR). During the years in which data were collected and analyzed, McKinley College was categorically deemed a tier-3, less-selective institution; however, it is also important to note that USNWR made several changes to their classification system for the 2011 "best college" rankings, based upon the Carnegie Classification system. USNWR now classifies schools within 2 tiers. Currently, USNWR only numerically ranks institutions classified as tier-1, or rather, those that fall

within the top 75 percent of their respective categories (National, Regional, etc.). Tier-2 schools are the lowest ranked (bottom 25 percent) within each respective category. According to USNWR, McKinley College is now categorized as a tier-two, selective, Regional College.

3.   In fact, the odds of making it out of high school and into higher education are greatly stacked against high school students affected by poverty. According to the National Center for Education Statistics, students from the lowest income quartile are ten times more likely to drop out of high school than their peers from the highest income quartile.

4.   See René Magritte's painting *The Treachery of Images* (1928-1929), which illustrates the concept of representation. As Magritte wrote beneath this now infamous image, "Ceci n'est pas une pipe" (This is not a pipe). Indeed, the image of a pipe is not a pipe, but the representation of a pipe.

5.   Vocational education is now often referred to as Career and Technical Education (CTE).

6.   Neoliberalism, as defined by Harvey (2005), is "a theory of political economic practices that proposes that human well-being can best be advanced by liberating individual entrepreneurial freedoms and skills within an institutional framework characterized by strong private property rights, free markets, and free trade" (p. 2) and its defining elements include "deregulation, privatization, and a withdrawal of the state from many areas of social provision" (p. 3).

7.   Stake (2005) addresses types of case studies, differentiating between intrinsic and instrumental cases. Intrinsic case studies research a particular, singular case for the sole purpose of understanding the particularity of the case itself; however, instrumental case studies examine a particular case to "provide insight into an issue or to redraw a generalization" (p. 445). In this case, McKinley and its museum are viewed in order to understand processes and their consequences within the larger system of higher education.

8.   According to Bourdieu, "a homology may be defined as a resemblance within a difference" (Bourdieu & Wacquant, 1992, p.106).

Chapter Two

Class, Knowledge, and Capital in Interrelated Contexts

Observable lines of connectivity run throughout this book, from one building to the next, from one neighborhood to another, and from one concept to the subsequent. Stepping back towards the far edges of the geographic and symbolic boundaries of the city of Arkive,[1] wherein this research takes place, allows for a perspective that includes a larger context in which to see the origins and formations of social inequalities. Stepping back even farther towards the outskirts of the system of higher education brings us closer to the logic of the organization and hierarchization of the system, the structure of knowledge, and the reproduction of inequality within the original structures from which we first stepped away.

This larger image of the social world of McKinley College, in relation to surrounding institutions, can be extended and traced outward using McKinley and the McKinley Museum of Art as the foci of a class-based geographic nexus of surrounding institutions. Extending the context beyond that of the college and museum to include the local, historical, and contemporary fields within which they are situated, helps to get at the intricacies and delicate subtleties of micro-level practices that maintain the circuit of reproduction within and across social institutions. Analyzed together, the former distinctions of micro and macro analyses disband their dualistic qualities under analytic union. Within the field of higher education, universities are not only "imbedded in complex relations of power with other universities" (Naidoo, 2004, p. 467), but they are also entrenched within a web of power relations with other educational and cultural institutions (e.g., art museums). Given the complexity of intersectionality among concepts and institutions to be addressed within this book, the purpose of this chapter can be simplified as one that is twofold. First, this chapter introduces the theoretical framework used

to make sense of the research presented in this book through Pierre Bourdieu's interrelated, core concepts as they operate within and across the system of higher education and the art world, relative to the production and
dissemination of elite knowledge. Secondly, this chapter locates and contex-
tualizes McKinley College and the McKinley Museum of Art within larger
fields to prepare the reader for the continuation of this analysis at the level of
the institutions and the people within them. This chapter's dual purpose
generates additional emphasis upon the book's underlying message of relational thinking in suggesting that these concepts and contexts are deeply
connected at the foundation of social inequality.

   To begin, this chapter reviews Bourdieu's relational constructs: field,
habitus, and capital (though in no way is this to be considered a thorough
overview of Bourdieu's complex analytic model), with particular attention to
the notion that knowledge itself is a specific form of capital across the fields
of higher education and the art world. The chapter then proceeds with a
discussion of the relationship between these two fields within the larger field
of power and ends by locating and contextualizing McKinley College and the
McKinley Museum of Art within their respective cross-cutting, interrelated
fields. Bourdieu's significant contributions to social reproduction and importantly, potential transformation (see Mills, 2008) advances concepts that remain essential to understanding the contemporary social condition in which
social stratification expands along with the system of higher education itself.

RELATIONALLY SPEAKING: FIELD, CAPITAL, AND HABITUS

Within his "genetic structuralism" (Bourdieu & Wacquant, 1992, p. 5) Bourdieu developed the foundational, interrelated conceptual tools field, capital,
and habitus, which taken together, reflect the heart of his relational approach
to sociology. Accordingly, Bourdieu brings together the often intellectually
isolated social (objective) and mental (subjective) structures of social space,
which he argues are "genetically linked" (p.13). In other words, rather than
separating structure and agent, or the objective from the subjective, Bourdieu
breaks with a sociological history of creating false antinomies through a
relational mode of thinking. For example, Bourdieu suggests that mental/
subjective structures and social/objective structures are mutually constitu-
tive—one cannot exist without the other. Relational thinking demands that
commonly held dualisms are fully understood only in light of each other—to
discuss habitus in the absence of cultural capital or cultural capital in the
absence of field is to construct an erroneous theoretical map surrounding the
contours of any social problem. Loïc Wacquant (2005), who has written
extensively on and with Bourdieu, writes: "The concepts of habitus, capital,

and field are thus internally linked to one another as each achieves its full analytical potency only in tandem with the others" (p. 9). Consider the notion of field. For Bourdieu: "To think in terms of field is to think relationally" (Bourdieu & Wacquant, 1992, p. 96). Each field follows its own particular logic and is defined by its own particular species of capital. According to Bourdieu,

> a field may be defined as a network, or a configuration, of objective relations between positions. These positions are objectively defined, in their existence and in the determinations they impose upon their occupants, agents or institutions, by their present and potential situation (situs) in the structure of the distribution of species of power (or capital) whose possession commands access to the specific profits that are at stake in the field, as well as by their objective relation to other positions (domination, subordination, homology, etc.). (Bourdieu & Wacquant, 1992, p. 97)

Bourdieu's conception of field emphasizes the objective structures that organize social space. Because these objective structures are limited and hierarchically situated positions, each field becomes a "battlefield" (Wacquant, 2005) wherein institutions and agents (people) struggle to accumulate particular forms of capital to compete for positions within that field. Positionality within any given field, then, depends upon the amount and type of capital accumulated. Relationally speaking, if Bourdieu's notion of field constitutes objective structures, then habitus constitutes the subjective. Boudieu's notion of habitus, a version of the older concept—one that can be traced back to Aristotle (Bourdieu & Wacquant, 1992; Reay, 2004), can be defined as "the system of durable and transposable dispositions through which we perceive, judge and act in the world" (Wacquant, 2005, p. 13). Individual habitus, for Bourdieu, combines one's past (e.g., familial upbringing) with one's present, but importantly, habitus is neither static nor fixed, but is "always in the process of completion" (Reay, 1998, p. 521). Again, Reay (1998) offers a clearer understanding of this incredibly complex concept: "It is primarily a dynamic concept, a rich interlacing of past and present, individual and collective, interiorized and permeating both body and psyche" (Reay, 1998, p. 521).

More collective notions of habitus, such as class habitus, for example, are important to an understanding of social positioning. Reay, David, and Ball (2005) suggest that this collective notion is "necessary . . . in order to recognize that individuals contain within themselves their past and present position in the social structure" (p. 25). Within the field of higher education, the concept institutional habitus (McDonough, 1997; Reay, 1998; Reay, David, & Ball, 2005) has been deemed valuable in making sense of the ways in which students from varying social class backgrounds "choose" institutions of higher education that reflect similar dispositions and values. In addition to school choice, ease of both navigation and immersion into particular types of institutions is often explained, in part, by consistencies between one's individual class-based habitus and the class-based habitus of the institution.

Within the field of higher education, Bourdieu identifies academic (also referred to as educational) capital as an "institutionalized form of cultural capital based on properties such as prior educational achievement, a 'disposition' to be academic (as observed, for example, in manner of speech and writing), and specially designated competencies" (Naidoo, 2004, p. 458). Within this book, dominant academic capital is often referred to as *elite knowledge*. This kind of knowledge "has consequences which are more than simply symbolic; it 'buys' prestige, power, and consequent economic positioning" (Grenfell & James, 1998, p. 22). Elite knowledge invites an educational discourse that favors a traditional liberal arts education—one that is largely dispensed in larger quantities within more prestigious institutions. The more academic capital one possesses, the more likely one is to attend and easily navigate prestigious institutions—those that place a high value upon particular types of knowledge. Privilege then begets privilege as individuals attending more prestigious institutions become further immersed into their elite cultures and later profit from their elite credentials. Relationally speaking, privilege constitutes the existence of under-privilege and under-privilege constitutes wealth, just as elite and non-elite constitute one another, wealth constitutes poverty, and poverty constitutes wealth. Simply, one cannot exist without the other. In this regard, students attending less prestigious institutions are offered different forms and quantities of academic capital—the "democratized" kind.

Using Bourdieu's well-conceived, though intentionally fuzzy and organic concept field allows for an understanding of the interrelated constructs habitus and capital as they function within McKinley College and the McKinley Museum of Art. This research, as approached from the analysis of two distinct but interrelated fields, becomes a complicated set of matrices that must resist simple reductionism and common antagonisms.

DEMOCRATIZING INTERRELATED FIELDS

Democratization has penetrated both higher education and the art world (particularly its institutionalized forms, e.g., art museums, university art history programs, and so forth) by seeping into a once impenetrable core and altering the face of elite knowledge as a form of cultural capital. Though not often considered together, these two fields are indeed homologous. Arguably, both higher education and the art world have largely resisted democratization while simultaneously changing their images and public discourses to those of access. The history, logic, and condition of both fields pull them together into view.

Art museums, an institutionalized part of the larger art world, have a longstanding and intimate relationship with universities. Historically, art museums and galleries have been of particular importance to the status of private liberal arts colleges, and more recently, these institutions have become fodder for public colleges and universities as they mimic private models of education (Duncan, 1993). When introduced in the nineteenth century, university galleries were built for educational and instructional purposes, and over time, burgeoned into the highly valued collections we know today—working to uphold and increase the status and prestige of the associated college and its local community. As the first to introduce the university art gallery in 1832, Yale afforded its art students the privilege of studying original artworks (Hoglund, 1984). But whether on or off university campuses, American art museums have a long history as producers of culture ("high culture")[2] and elite knowledge, and more recently, both have demonstrated the desire to democratize. Since their early inception, art museums, operating within and in conjunction with a larger social network of other cultural and educational institutions (universities/colleges), have established certain forms of knowledge as legitimate and reproduce cultural ideologies that ultimately act as exclusionary devices for the privileged (Bourdieu, 1984, 1993; DiMaggio, 1978; Duncan, 1993). Alan Wallach (2002), who has written extensively on art museums, reminds us of the rather harsh reluctance of these institutions to disband from a deeply elitist history:

> Theses institutions may have felt obliged to open their doors to visitors of whatever stripe or background, but they did not believe they were duty-bound to make such visitors feel particularly welcome. . . . The museum became for many a forbidding or bewildering place. (p.104)

After opening their doors to a broader audience, art museums attracted record-setting numbers of visitors with the hugely popular, corporate-funded, blockbuster exhibition. The blockbuster forever changed museums and, in part, their audiences. College-educated professionals and college-going youth composed this new audience that would consume original artworks and their heavily marketed reproductions upon leaving the exhibition's final stop: the museum store—another space influenced by corporate reorganization. In sensing the speed of capitalism (Agger, 1989), museums began altering their infrastructures to more closely model the corporations that were now funding exhibitions. These changes included, among other things, the establishment of marketing, education, membership, and publication departments (Wallach, 2002)—all of which simultaneously created new career opportunities within higher education. Wallach (2002) further makes this connection clear:

> The age of the Blockbuster marked the dramatic expansion of the American art museum's audience and at the same time the reorganization and expansion of major art museums along modern corporate lines. The new public that began to appear at art museums in the 1960s was attracted by a new phenomenon that the media eventually called 'the blockbuster' exhibition. Not surprisingly, the rise of this new audience coincided with the rapid growth of American higher education that began in the 1950s, and along with it the spread of standardized introductory art history courses. (Wallach, 2002, p. 119)

With a focus on greater outreach, the use of strategies that appeal to a more diverse audience, and increasing museum attendance, it would appear that art museums have successfully democratized, transcending their elitist origins. In fact, public art museums are among the most heavily visited cultural institutions and have become one of the most popular venues for entertainment, even in 2009 during the recession, visitor attendance either remained steady or was on the rise in American art museums (Goldstein, 2009). This settles well with the American art museum's more democratic approach to issues of accessibility and education. But who exactly are these visitors? Wallach (2002) suggests an interesting and much-overlooked detail regarding this increase: "The demographics of museum visitors have probably not substantially changed over the last 20 years or so, it is rather the frequency with which about 20 percent of the population visits art museums that accounts for the increase" (p. 114). Those visitors are still largely the middle and upper-middle class, white, and college-educated. DiMaggio and Useem (1978) noted decades ago that "blue-collar workers, individuals with low incomes or little education, and racial and ethnic minorities are found to be greatly underrepresented" (p. 179).

Not unlike art museums, the system of higher education today appears to operate under a very similar democratic logic—increasing numbers of admissions among minority students and students from lower socio-economic backgrounds seemingly results in an overall reduction in inequality. The connections between art museums and higher education are pronounced, but we know very little about the ways in which art museums associated with colleges/universities move both with and among two seemingly separate worlds. Together, the fields of higher education and the art world offer a discourse of democratized knowledge for a public lacking access to more privileged sites. Part of this process to democratize education and offer equal educational opportunities is in the democratization of elite knowledge (making the fine arts, literature, theater, among other "high" forms of knowledge and culture, more accessible) and the absorption of more elite cultural capital. However, we know the system of higher education today, indeed offering more opportunity, is far from being a vision of equal access, opportunity, and outcome. As closely connected to the field of higher education and its discontents, the art world, too, is arguably far from being democratized. When operating within and in association with colleges and universities, art museums, together with other social institutions and social forces acting upon them, help to maintain class divisions through the reproduction of elite knowledge, ideology, power, and privilege.

Though particular species of capital are field-specific, academic capital circulates throughout the art world and higher education, in addition to other shared forms of symbolic and cultural capital. The visual arts, as a form of elite knowledge (academic capital), can be located within both fields of higher education and the art world (wherein art historians are trained). These institutions work together to legitimize elite knowledge (and its democratization), affording all students and visitors, regardless of background, with equal opportunities to absorb and accumulate highly valued academic capital. While the once distinct binary between the "high arts" and "low arts" may have become fuzzy with the age of the blockbuster, corporatization, and consumer saturation (Collins, 2002), so too has the distinct binary between what might be deemed "elite" and "practical" knowledge. The visual arts, as part of an elite, liberal arts education, have permeated across various fields to preserve power under the discourse of access and democratization. As part of these interconnected fields, the Rust Belt city of Arkive and its educational and culture-producing institutions hold a particularly precarious position, again, one common to other similarly positioned US cities.

ARKIVE'S RUSTED URBAN LANDSCAPE

The nation's Rust Belt summons images of post-industrialization, poverty, emptiness, neglected space, crumbling architectures, piles of wreckage, and the half-buried sediments of the past—"the ghastliness of failed utopias" (Crichlow, 2003)—and the decline of a rusted urban landscape. Many Rust Belt cities continue to struggle to improve their aesthetic, economic, and social conditions to preempt further decline and resultant waves of human departure (more than half of the population disappeared from its geographic borders over the course of six decades of decline within Arkive, New York). In the 1950s, Arkive's population peaked at 580,000, and in 2008, it fell to its lowest number of inhabitants since the 1800s. In 2008, 28.7 percent of its total population was living below the poverty line and the 2009 Department of Labor indicates the unemployment rate to have reached 9 percent. Arkive's poverty, like most larger American cities, is concentrated in its metropolitan core, spilling into surrounding areas, pushing the geographic boundaries of poverty, marred by severe racial segregation. In 2012, Arkive holds its position as one of the poorest cities in the nation, and one of the most racially segregated. "White flight" in Arkive, like so many other U.S. cities, has shifted the once white majority to a growing outer suburban ring. While Arkive's total metro population decreased by roughly half of its peak over fifty years, surrounding suburbs doubled and tripled in population. Arkive's predominantly Black urban core, living in the greatest degree of poverty, designates the severity of de facto segregation. The racially charged movement of white individuals and families segregates by color and by class, though these two constructions are difficult, if not impossible, to isolate. Arkive's metropolitan center is, simply, a testament to the ways in which race and class are so tightly bound. A 2007 *New York Times* article depicts Arkive as "beaten down" by "residential exodus" and decades of deindustrialism. On tree-lined urban streets, abandoned houses and dilapidated buildings indicate the crisis of this extreme exodus—a striking contrast between prospering natural life and artificial death. Factories and plants, formerly alive, have been leveled, or exist as industrialized remains balanced on the edge of a history of a once thriving economy. Despite efforts to revitalize, these statistics and images of deterioration, neglect, and poverty, which further generate images of crime, fearful residents, and other social ills, manifest into generalized, symbolic representations of a city and its people. The persistence of an overwhelming sense of "working class-ness" pervades Arkive's deindustrialized core, demarcating the changing color of images of the "working class"—from that of the white, male, factory worker, to the Black, urban, and working-poor. The changing "rust belt" landscape and the collective consciousness defining the "working-class" today gather within the space of declining Arkive, presenting distorted images fraught with historic reference and contemporary race- and class-based fear.

CLASS CONTRAST IN ARKIVE

Bordered by the College's newly freestanding art museum, an internationally renowned art museum, and a neighboring history museum, McKinley and the McKinley Museum of Art are positioned at the center of what is known in Arkive as the cultural district—a rich network of cultural and educational institutions. The manifestation of wealth within these cultural institutions and the corresponding concentrations of personal wealth starkly contrast surrounding neighborhoods, some of which are separated only by a considerable block, often marked by racially-drawn lines and a significant drop in income. The campus is situated at the center of this local nexus. Positioned on Main

Street, McKinley faces the International Museum of Art (IMA), located directly across the street. The International Museum, built during a time of great prosperity, has transformed through times of economic struggle, but along the length of its own history, has remained an institution of international recognition. The museum adorns Main Street with a great white physicality in marble and stone. As a hybrid building (with a visibly stark architectural divide between the original building and the modern expansion), the museum still appears today to display the wealth and distinction of its founders. The original structure, built around the turn of the twentieth century, emerged as a model of Greek revival through the philanthropic efforts of one wealthy contributor. Marble columns and an impressive, though rather imposing façade, gave the appearance of civility and distinction—what many consider an elite presence with an exclusionary aura. In 1960, the museum expanded and this addition was designed in the tradition of the "modernist cube"—a contemporary design to the times and adding to the original floor plan to accommodate its burgeoning collection of modern and contemporary art.

To McKinley's south side, though part of the campus, stands the newly built, 84,000 square-foot, contemporary architecture of the McKinley Museum of Art. To the immediate north, an elevated highway rolls around its core, partially circumscribing the campus. To its western-most end, the campus is bordered by rows of low-income housing and a community center with high metal fencing, the location of much of the city's early ethnic neighborhoods. This vision sits opposite the 5,000 tons of marble assembled into the neoclassical architecture of the International Museum of Art thinly bordered by roads lined with some of the most expensive real estate in the city. Situated between such economic disparity, McKinley and its museum are positioned in the middle of visible class contrast. This positionality imposes lines of symbolic and geographic connectivity that help to conceal important class disconnections and distances.

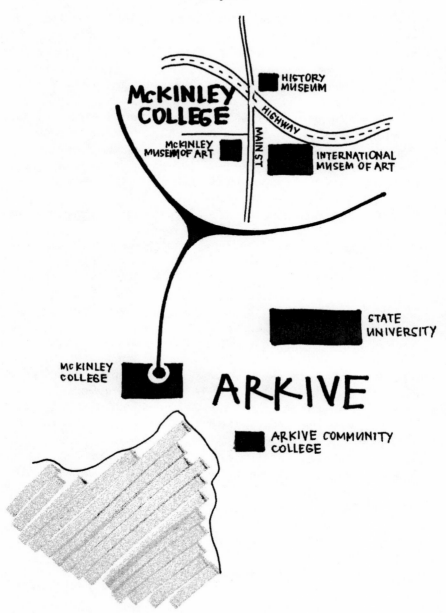

Figure 2.1.   Hand drawn map of Arkive courtesy of Robin Boyko.

Connected not only by proximity, McKinley College and the surrounding local, cultural and educational institutions share a circuit of common social agents that preserve the field through its various (dominant) positions. It is perhaps not surprising that the President of McKinley is a former member of the Board of Directors at the International Museum of Art (IMA) or that certain staff members at the McKinley Museum of Art were formerly employed by the IMA, or that the two buildings share the same volunteer docents, or that staff members at the McKinley Museum of Art also teach classes at McKinley College. Given the immediate geographic proximity, these joint positions and social connections seem entirely natural and expected; however, these connections conceal class-based disconnections revealed only when Bourdieu's concepts and the local context are combined.

This chapter describes an invisible force field where both individual, class-based, and institutional habitus often conflict. The differentiation of forms of capital, types of knowledge, and an ensemble of dispositions run between McKinley College and other cultural institutions, particularly the IMA (perhaps the most culturally elite of local institutions). This force field accentuates opposing terms and conditions. The width of just one street separates these institutions, one considered within the local context as 'working class' and the other 'elite.' Though the IMA, like much of the art world today, subscribes to a discourse of access, the community perception of it does not always reinforce the merit of such discourse. Mark, a retired McKinley art history professor, recounts the general perceptions of his students:

> The first day of class I would ask if they had been to the IMA and just a few hands would go up, mostly art students. So, I always had this one assignment that would get them over there and they might really like it. A lot of them, I was surprised . . . this was something I didn't understand because growing up in Washington going to museums was something you did. As a child, my father used to take me all the time. It just seemed like a natural thing. But I found that younger students felt uneasy about going to the IMA. It's an art museum, and they weren't really welcome. It was just an impression, but it wasn't true [they did not feel welcome, but he feels that they are welcome and should not feel this way]. It was an elitist place [students said this] . . . I found that kind of funny. I said, "well, that's not true. The lunches are good and they're not real expensive." But there was that sense that was kind of the old [city] mentality and this is uptown, the working didn't go to museums . . . that was something for the well to do, the mansion dwellers. I found that unusual.

Though intersections of knowledge, buildings, and people connect and create positions, often illuminating unequal social structure, they also reinforce notions of the seemingly natural construction of social reality. Data presented in following chapters suggest that McKinley students do not visit the IMA. Of course, the reasons for these absences are far more complicated than the simple notion that these students share a collective disinterest in the visual arts (Bourdieu, 1993).

Because McKinley College is geographically located between these institutions and symbolically juxtaposed through comparative discourse, it cannot be analyzed without an understanding of the relational institutional positions within the immediate context of Arkive. This becomes perhaps most evident through a comparative discourse of surrounding colleges and universities that shapes McKinley's institutional identity. In forthcoming chapters, data reveal that McKinley is often held in contradistinction to State University, a larger, multi-campus institution (the most sizable part of the school is located in a middle-class suburb of Arkive). According to *U.S. News and World Report*, State University, a large public four-year comprehensive research university, ranks among the top 150 tier-1 institutions. As a "more selective" institution, McKinley is often cast in the shadow of State University. When McKinley is not discussed relative to State University, it is paired against or discussed as similar to Arkive Community College, located in Arkive's downtown core. Arkive Community College is a two-year junior college enrolling more than 27,000 students across one urban and two suburban campuses. These comparisons, in conjunction with history and social process, shape the identity of McKinley College.

MCKINLEY COLLEGE AND THE MCKINLEY MUSEUM OF ART

It has been more than a decade since I first set foot on the campus of McKinley College. My parents dropped me off after helping to unload a minivan full of the materials of my adolescence. In 2008, I again walked on to McKinley campus to study the very context of my undergraduate education. The campus did not reflect the wrinkles and wear accumulated by the lapse of time, but instead reflected transformation and progress. I had missed the way the urban air circulated through these particular academic buildings and the familiar feel of my lungs restricting while climbing the stairs of the campus library. I noticed things missing, like the centrally placed fountain that sprayed a fine mist across the campus in the summers and ice during the brutality of Northeast winters. I assumed administration had had enough of students injecting the water with dye. The dormitory where I had lived was still standing tall—the College's first high-rise residential building, built in the early sixties. I always found this building to be anything but aesthetically pleasing—its exterior had not changed. Perhaps routine maintenance had preserved this austere, unattractive structure. I noticed new additions to the Student Union and wished the food had been different years ago. My stomach ached. Indeed, things were both familiar and strange. Visiting McKinley felt like running into an old friend you have not seen in years, passing through waves of nostalgia, and picking up exactly where you left off. This nostalgia, however, is not the only reason McKinley seemed appropriate for my research purposes.

McKinley College was chosen as a singular case because it represents the kind of institution Duncan (1993) refers to as one that is "democratized," but also because of its unique location within a social network of cultural and educational institutions (considered elite within the local community), including the McKinley Museum of Art, because of its emphasis on the visual arts (as a democratized form of elite knowledge), and its reputation as a working class institution (to be discussed in chapters to follow). McKinley College, part of the State system of public higher education, enrolls one of the largest numbers of students and is also one of the largest comprehensive four-year institutions in the system. As a less selective, public institution, McKinley is to be understood, within this research, as a product of the democratization of higher education. According to the Carnegie Classification System, McKinley is considered a medium-sized school that is predominantly non-residential, with a higher student transfer-in rate. 2008 statistics (when this research was conducted) indicate that McKinley's student body is relatively diverse in terms of race, ethnicity, and age. Of the roughly 11,000 students enrolled in both undergraduate and graduate programs (163 undergraduate majors and 63 graduate programs), a percentile breakdown of the student body for 2008 is largely comprised of Caucasian (74.6 percent) and African American (14.7 percent) students, while 1.5 percent identify as Asian, 5.3 percent identify as Hispanic, and 0.3 percent as Native American. 58 percent of undergraduate students in 2008 were from the same county in which McKinley is located. The majority of McKinley undergraduates are between the ages of 20 and 21, followed by 18 and19, which is then closely followed by students between the ages of 22 and 24. This suggests a rather large percentage of older or non-traditional students. In addition to these statistics, rates of retention, the number of full-time students, the percentage of full-time students working, and graduation rates (as well as other facts of this nature) are among statistics collected by the institution for public review, but offer very little for determining a traditionally defined set of classifications of social class for this student body. As a commonly used proxy for socioeconomic status, first-generation status and percentage of Pell grant recipients are important to the classification of McKinley and its students. By way of example, Freie and Bratt (2009) use first-generation status as an indicator of students' "working-class" identity:

> First generation and working class are categories which, while unique, are often connected by a shared cultural and economic background and our definitions of these categories come from the literature addressing working-class identity. (Freie & Bratt, pp. 3-4)

McKinley, a college with a high percentage of first-generation undergraduate students (according to McKinley College's Office of Financial Aid, 48 percent of students for the 2007-2008 school year identified as first-generation), constitutes, in this study, a largely working-class student body and is considered a "working-class institution." A 2005 study of first-generation students recorded "almost 30 percent of first-generation students come from homes with annual family income under 25,000, compared to 9.2 percent of non-first-generation students" (Capriccioso, 2006, p. 1). In addition, it was not entirely surprising to find that 58 percent of McKinley undergraduate students qualified for Pell in 2007-2008. For the sake of perspective, the national average for Pell grant recipients for 2007-2008 was 27 percent (NCES).

In terms of campus culture, the visual arts are key to the school's enrichment objectives and capture some of the most interesting attributes of this working class college. In addition to the Fine Arts Department, the student gallery, and various programs in the arts (including one of the nation's oldest programs in art education and a smattering of artwork on view throughout the campus), McKinley made a significant investment in a rich collection of regional artworks for public view, establishing the McKinley Museum of Art. In March of 2008, the museum closed its location in one of the oldest buildings on the campus and re-opened in a new building at the fore of the campus, directly opposite the International Museum of Art. Though the new building is visible from the street, the entrance reveals an interesting, and arguably important, architectural decision, as it is turned away from the street towards the interior of the campus.[3] Aesthetically, this building was not constructed to blend into the architecture of the campus—it is, in fact, more of an abstract sculpture than a "building." In other words, the architecture alone does not draw an immediate visual relationship to the campus. According to the architect's website, the building was intended to reference other local architectural structures—those set within the surrounding cultural district—all within walking distance. The museum bends around the edge of the campus while mimicking the International Museum in its rotunda-style ground plan. Inside, the museum is a dramatic, open space, intended to be "dynamic, varied and unexpected."[4] The museum offers educational programs (e.g. art classes), more formal spaces for learning, and docent-led tours of the collection. Although the museum is considered a stand-alone structure, seemingly separate and distinct, it remains in affiliation with and geographically tied to the college campus. Its distinction as a 501c3 classifies the museum as an autonomous, independent organization that allows for association and collaboration with McKinley College.

The urban location of the campus, one that resides at the center of the city's cultural district, geographically announces its position within a network of cultural institutions (exemplified by its position adjacent to an internationally renowned art museum) and has become an important part of its internal structure. For example, the College's promotional materials (e.g. website and brochures to attract prospective students) are woven with reference to the relevance of the College's location among the cultural district. Surrounded by a world-class art museum, galleries, and icons of local architecture, McKinley is indeed situated within a unique cultural nexus (one that is undercut by an equally unique socioeconomic nexus). The relationships between these institutions are important to the sociological analysis to follow and are further discussed within subsequent chapters. In vacillating from larger fields to their institutions and back again, we now move inside of McKinley, a working-class college.

NOTES

1. Arkive is a chosen pseudonym for the city in which this research was conducted. The spelling of Arkive, as an intentional misspelling of the word "archive," is meant to subtly announce the image, breadth, and meaning of the familiar term (archive). As a noun, an archive evokes the image of a dimly-lit vault buried under towering boxes of documented history. But archives take on various shapes and sizes—they are both vast and concrete spaces (Bachelard, 1994). They are spaces of "intimate immensity" (Bachelard, 1994). McKinley College itself is an archive—a space that is the collection of images, memories, and social-psychological depth. The McKinley Museum of Art is perhaps a more literal archive in the documentation of the past, and the city itself is an archive of sorts. It is a time capsule with meaning at every turn. But to get inside this archive requires a break with the dialectics of inside and outside, a break which "confers spatiality upon thought" (Bachelard, 1994, p. 212). Arkive is, then, a term for a space that is both vast and concrete and requires the excavation of both mental and social structures.

2. The concept of "high" versus "low" culture is no longer very useful due to the proliferation and cultural saturation of what is "popular." High and low are also viewed here as false dichotomies, something Bourdieu tries to both diminish and transcend in *The Field of Cultural Production* (1993).

3. The distinctive architecture and aesthetic appearance of the McKinley Museum of Art are concealed for the purpose of anonymity as describing the unique appearance of the museum would risk revealing its identity.

4. This quotation is taken from the architect's webpage; however, the identity and site remain anonymous to ensure the anonymity of the campus.

Chapter Three

Reputational *Affects:* Inside a Working Class College

The eyes of others our prisons; their thoughts our cages.
—Virginia Woolf, Monday or Tuesday, An Unwritten Novel, 1921

Virginia Woolf was right; human perception is a confining space and its boundaries difficult to escape. Though dominant images and definitions of the working classes have changed slightly throughout history and across location, residual reputational effects of these dominant conceptions continue to hold a particular stigma within the changing context of higher education. As Reay (2001) argues, "we cannot talk about working-class relationships to education without examining dominant representations of the working classes" (p. 335). Reay continues: "In Bourdieurian terms, the working classes both historically and currently are constituted as an unknowing, un-critical, tasteless mass from which the middle class draw their distinctions" (Skeggs, 2000, p. 335). Reay, who has written extensively, and brilliantly, on social class and higher education within the UK, argues that this association (negatively) affects the development of students' academic/learner identities, in part, because of dominant historical and contemporary depictions of the working classes. These dominant representations imbue the working classes with reputations of inferiority and intellectual deficit—the residual effects of historical misrepresentation.

Not unlike the UK, images and judgments of the working classes within the US are also caught up in a collective of eyes and minds—reflecting the very same pathologized representations of the working class and shaping individual and institutional reputation. Mike Rose (2004) best articulates these associations and residual effects in the American context as he asserts: "This kind of generalizing, this slippage of assumptions, runs through our

29

cultural history, from post-Revolutionary War mechanics who were por-
trayed as illiterate and incapable of participating in government to the auto-
workers I heard labeled by one supervisor as 'a bunch of dummies'" (pp. xxi-
xxii). A great deal of scholarship within both countries has observed the
working class as "outsiders to higher education" (Bourdieu, in Reay, p. 336).
Whitty (2001) argues: "From the work of Flaud to Halsey in the 1950s
onwards (Halsey et al. 1961), the dominant concern has been with working-
class failure" (p. 287). To be working class then, immediately distinguishes
individuals (and institutions) as substandard and counter to the culture of
higher education. This belabored reputation of the working class follows
students into higher education and reaches well into the twenty-first century,
producing *affects* that contribute to the reproduction of social inequality.

This chapter, then, contributes to enhancing our understanding of the
reputational *affects* of social class status relative to higher education. Arguably situated somewhere within Kathleen Stewart's (2007) poetic conception
of "ordinary affects"—the "public feelings that begin and end in broad circulation," but also "the stuff that seemingly intimate lives are made of" (Stewart, 2007, p. 2), reputational *affects* cannot be located through the more
common statistical calculation of reputational *effects*. Rather, reputational
affects are the deeply felt, socially constructed components of everyday
life—they are more the sticky residues left behind by the constancy of reputation than reputation itself—the stuff that leaves a lasting mark and won't
wash clean or easily shake free. As a supplement to existing qualitative and
quantitative research that seeks to identify an independent effect gained by
attending a prestigious university (Strathdee, 2009), this research not only
seeks to identify the more tangible effects of reputation, but also the less
quantifiable *affects* accumulated through attending a less-prestigious university (one with a weaker reputation). Not unlike Stewart's 'ordinary affects,'
"They happen in impulses, sensations, expectations, daydreams, encounters,
and habits of relating . . . and in publics and social worlds of all kinds that
catch people up in something that feels like *something*" (2007, p. 2). A firmer
description depends upon the field within which *affects* are felt and reputation is lived out. This chapter brings that *something* elusive into view and
offers up a more definitive form of reputational *affects* through emblematic
excerpts of interviews with McKinley students, faculty, staff, and administration. These interviews simultaneously reveal and reproduce the social construction of McKinley's working-class reputation while baring the resultant
reputational *affects* that resemble the image of stigmatized *working class*
outsiders within higher education. This resemblance, of course, is not without its own contemporary twist. Though the unfavorable reputation of the
working classes pervades education today and retains a certain historical
quality, it presents a slightly different appearance—one redressed by time
and an expanding, differentiated context of higher education.

Steeped in a *sense* of reality, the construction of McKinley as a "working class" college, buttressed by images and notions of the working class as the lacking, intellectually and culturally inferior masses of higher education, assembles the syntax of McKinley's "rusted" reputation. The order and structure of the language of this rusted space lifts a durable social narrative into view—one that discursively orders and structures the space within which it circulates. This narrative invades public and private contexts and solidifies the reputations of both institutions and individuals within them, while further structuring the social language applied to and conveyed within these spaces. But before feeling out the structures of reputational *affect*, the question remains: Just how durable is this concept?

A SOCIOLOGY OF "RUSTED" REPUTATION

Reputation building is part of existing social process; in fact, reputation building has taken on new speed in an era of enhanced competition. As a form of capital, reputation can exceedingly limit or permit privilege. It can become immovable, impermeable, and fixed in one form, but then mutate, slowly giving way to a new identity. It inhabits a charged, social-psychological space, and it follows closely, moving as a shadow—an image that is at once closely representative and yet slightly distorted. Reputation building, however, is not unidirectional—it builds in equal measure up and down the length of a status scale. As Rodden (2006) notes: "Reputation emerges from a complex of factors, both historical and social. Reputation and value are contingent and not correlative concepts . . . Reputation is not a matter of ability, nor is it merely a matter of 'chance,' but rather of positioning . . . One needs to see the rise of reputation less as a question of luck and more as a matter of distinctive historical and social location" (p. 76). The fall of reputation then, like its rise, would also seem to be a matter of distinctive historical and social location. Indeed, when we consider the city's historical decline, and its social location within the competitive global economy, it seems isolated and bound to an unfortunate reputation (even if this reputation begins to turn back and rise, this process is one that can be staggeringly slow). But, as Emler (1990) argues, "reputations are also judgments, about vices and virtues, strengths and weaknesses, based on accumulating patterns of evidence which societies constantly process and reprocess" (p. 178). Judgments, paired with the accumulation of "facts" (history, rank, etc.), converge in conversations, forming reputations over time (Emler, 1990), the good and the bad.

The reputations that seem to catch the attention of scholars (and the general public), however, are typically the good. Within sociology, and sociology of education in particular, literature on reputation tends to ignore institutions of education with poor reputations, while focusing on the reputational effects of attending institutions with considerable prestige—typically those with long-standing, elite reputations. In other words, reputation, as applied within higher education, is often synonymous with institutions that have only "the best" reputations—those that evoke the highly favorable, pristine images of the Ivy League and those that lead their graduates into similarly prestigious, reputable positions within the occupational structure. Few scholars study reputation from the opposite end of the Ivy, and fewer examine the role of reputation in the process of social reproduction.

In an effort to advance reputation as a central concept deserving of increased scrutiny, Robert Strathdee (2009) offers a comprehensive take on how the concept has been applied within the field of sociology of education to date. Though Strathdee is researching reputation within the context of the United Kingdom, his argument and direction could not be more timely or relevant to the United States, a nation that continues to experience the effects (and affects) of the democratization and expansion of higher education, namely, increasing stratification. Following Bourdieu, the author informs us that institutional reputation is indeed a form of capital (linked to institutional and individual habitus) and a feature of social reproduction within the field of higher education. More specifically, reputation, as a form of capital and as part of institutional habitus, is tightly bound to curriculum and "the expressive order of institutions" (attitudes toward learning, expectations, demeanor, and so forth). Reay et al. (2010) argue: "They (the expressive order) constitute embodied cultural capital—embodied in the collectivity of students, in their dress, demeanor and attitudes, in particular, their attitudes towards learning and their degree of confidence and entitlement in relation to academic knowledge" (p. 3). As embodied, reputation produces great *affect*. Indeed, and as demonstrated by the research to follow, reputation is formed and maintained through social discourse; however, reputation has received little consideration as a form of capital, as part of a dominant discourse that structures social reality, and as a powerful, durable concept contributing to social reproduction.

Within the larger system of higher education, the process of reputation "building" through the circulation of discourse within and between institutions makes these spaces increasingly resistant to transformation (less susceptible to change, and thereby, less susceptible to improved reputation). Weaker reputations built upon notions of inferiority and inadequacy are then buttressed by arbitrary systems of rank and prestige. Though reputation becomes embodied and personified, it is never tactile. Even as it passes freely into permeable space through these arbitrary systems and discursive practices that accumulate and converge over time to produce real social consequences, it cannot be moved or held, pushed away, or covered up. Reputation has endurance, the kind that leaves behind a long historical line of constructed social reality.

CONSTRUCTING MCKINLEY'S WORKING CLASS REPUTATION

> Like I have younger siblings. I have a sister that's 19, a brother that's 18, and a sister that's 16 and my mother would not send them in a million years to McKinley. She was really pissed off that I could not get into State University. She was angry. She was really mad. But I don't care, I was rebellious and I think that the population stems from people who have that same mentality, like, isn't it great that you're going to McKinley? And it is great, but then you have people from "Status Woods" who would never in a million years send their kids to McKinley.
> —Rachel, Faculty of Education

Rachel is a fairly new, full-time faculty member at McKinley College and also attended McKinley as an undergraduate student. Above, Rachel reflects on her mother's negative feelings toward the College and, within these pages, begins to shape the class-based discourse of McKinley. With a distinct sense of loyalty to McKinley, Rachel defends the school through her own individual act of "rebellion," attending McKinley against her mother's wishes. Her mother, who experienced late class mobility through a second marriage to a man who moved the family to "Status Woods,"[1] was angry that her daughter was not accepted to State University. For Rachel's mother, State University is more prestigious—it is good enough for her daughter. McKinley, however, seems to lack a certain something—so much so that it inspired feelings of anger and provoked Rachel's sense of rebellion as she enrolled as an undergraduate student, even though McKinley was her only option. Rachel's defense of McKinley also reveals a common comparison, significant to the maintenance of McKinley's reputation. On several occasions, McKinley and its students were mentioned in opposition to State University. State University, a higher-ranking, research-one institution, with a considerable graduate population, is positioned against McKinley in rank, but also in terms of social class (of its students and as an institution). Surprisingly though, the percentage of first-generation students at State University (47 percent) is nearly equal to that of McKinley (48 percent). These statistics, though arguably more complex than they appear,[2] demonstrate the strength of socially constructed spaces. Relative to State University, McKinley is the inferior institution, the institution that is not good enough for the children of "Status Woods." More dramatically stated, it is an institution that "people

from Status Woods would never in a million years send their kids to."
Through this conversation, Rachel reveals a class-based opposition to
McKinley and begins to expose the tenuous relationship between the working class and higher education. Though Rachel herself attended McKinley,
she highlights its poor reputation in the minds and eyes of the middle class
(of Status Woods) whose opposition (in the case of her mother) dips to an
emotional depth, while also bringing attention to the hierarchical positioning
of institutions. Even as these two institutions serve a student body whose
class background appears more similar than different, they are solidly positioned against each other by way of oppositional reputations. As a proxy for
quality, reputation seems to maintain the positioning of these two institutions
within the field of higher education.

As Rachel and I further discuss McKinley, she tells me why she thinks
students choose this school:

> AS: Why do you imagine students choose McKinley College?
> R: Education students come to McKinley because it's cheap and it's a good
> education. It has the reputation for being a good, affordable education school.
> So it's still looked at as a teacher's college so the education students definitely
> come here for that reason. The rest of the students I think they come in
> because . . . if you're from . . . I get a lot of students from [rural suburb of city]
> and those students, because of . . . I think it's because of the culture of where
> they live that they, you know, because it is more of a working class model
> where they live.

Rachel, like other faculty members with whom I spoke, suggests that many
students attend McKinley because the working-class culture of the school
compliments their working-class upbringing. This would certainly support
research that argues students will "choose" postsecondary institutions where
they feel they "belong" (Bourdieu, 1990; Reay et al., 2010). Scholarship also
indicates that students from disadvantaged or working-class backgrounds
often have difficulty navigating the space of higher education as one that
promotes middle-class values (Aries & Seider, 2005; Horvat & Antonio,
1999) and "valorizes middle- rather than working-class cultural capital"
(Reay, 2001, p. 334). With few exceptions (Leathwood & O'Connel, 2003;
Reay et al., 2010), these studies typically reference the difficulties expressed
through hybridized identities of poor and working-class students within more
elite institutions of higher education (Baxter & Brinton, 2001). But, as scholars continue to largely ignore the experiences of students within less prestigious institutions, the system of higher education becomes increasingly sizable (for both the US and UK, in particular), and increasingly competitive.
While the majority of working-class and minority students attend less prestigious institutions, students from middle-class backgrounds are slowly (and
for some, begrudgingly) enrolling in less prestigious colleges and univer-

sities. In short, it seems there is still much to be learned. For example, what about students who feel more like "fish out of water" within "working class" schools? Consider Ava, a fourth-year art history student, enrolled in McKinley's Honors Program:

> A: I mean I don't hate it, but actually McKinley was not my first choice. I did NOT want to go to McKinley. That was my safety school that I applied to because they had the art program in the area. I mean, honestly, if I could speak frank, it is very ghetto at McKinley as opposed to State University and I don't particularly appreciate that because I am not from that. I went to school with a bunch of other Catholics and I am used to everyone being very proper, not ignorant.
> AS: Can you tell me what you mean by that?
> A: I try not to hold judgment, but okay. Working class Arkive means probably a lot of the time, students are more worried about making their car payment, bills, their tuition, than they are their grades. It is like, let's be honest here, McKinley college is a working class, is a blue-collar school for the most part. Unfortunately, that sometimes has an effect on a lot of students that they are not as engaged in class. They think "it is just school, I will get it over with." It is not a time for them to really explore and discover something new about themselves. It is hard to critically think and to write, *I* am still battling with it, but *I* enjoy it.

In this passage, Ava makes the explicit association between being working class and demonstrating a lack of intellectual engagement. She describes her experience at McKinley by comparing herself to her peers in a way that distinguishes her as someone who "enjoys" thinking and learning, as opposed to the other students, who she refers to as working class, who do not conceive of thinking and learning in the same way or with the same level of engagement. From Ava's perspective, these students have other priorities to which she cannot relate—priorities that supersede more intellectual pursuits.

The institutional habitus of McKinley is evidenced by discursive patterns of working class students, but this can also be understood relationally, through the decidedly middle-class students who feel 'othered' by their working-class peers. For example, the few middle-class students I interviewed at McKinley (given parental education-level and occupation, for example, one or both parents attended post-secondary school and had traditional middle-class occupations such as nurse, teacher, mechanical engineer) seemed to struggle with the kind of hybridized identity that has been typically used to describe working-class students attending elite institutions. Though not the same set of tensions exist for many working-class students attending elite institutions, these middle class students at McKinley expressed a very clear sense of the unfamiliar and an inherent unsettledness within this working class institution and amongst their working class peers. As Reay et al. (2009) assert: "[w]hen habitus encounters a field with which it is not familiar, the resulting disjunctures can generate not only change and transformation, but also disquiet, ambivalence, insecurity and uncertainty" (p. 1105). These middle class students within a working class institution seem to have found themselves within a context that incites something more like disgust than ambivalence; an identity less than hybridized, but more one that retains a stronghold on middle classness.

This grip on one's middle classness is also implicated in the amount of time spent on campus. Ava has never lived on campus, much like other students who seem to come from similar middle-class backgrounds. Sara, also a commuter student and decidedly middle class, says she enjoys the campus, but lives at her parent's suburban home and spends very little time engaging in campus culture:

> S: I commute here, so I still live with my two younger sisters at home. I live in the suburbs . . . very quiet and safe.
> AS: And how much time do you spend here?
> S: I just commute here and I don't spend much time here not in class, other than occasionally for a theater production, I don't come here unless for school.

Sara, who sounds more like a campus visitor spending time only in classes, communicates a sense of alienation and frustration with "the typical McKinley College student." Her sentiments are reflected in the physical distance she maintains between her life outside of class and campus—the opposite of her "quiet and safe" suburban lifestyle. However, middle-class residential students also communicate a sense of frustration with peers and a difficulty relating. Amanda, a second-year, middle class student:

> AS: So you've had a little bit of experience; can you talk about your experience so far at McKinley?
> A: It's honestly, I'd say I'm a pessimist so this might be bad, but it just seems everything there is mediocre. Like everything, just the service with everything, you look at the quality of everything . . . very mediocre. Of course, you're not asking for much because it's McKinley, it's not really the best. It's discouraging to see the dorms aren't filled with the best people.

Here, Amanda expresses distaste for her peers—"they are not the best people," which to her seems to follow a certain logic because, as she mentions, "McKinley isn't really the best." This sentiment is communicated throughout interviews with both students and faculty, revealing McKinley's lackluster reputation in terms of academic standards, lack of rigor, unmotivated student body, and professors who "just want to push students through."

A CREDENTIAL DISPENSING INSTITUTION

Michael, a working-class, non-traditional, transfer student who started higher education at a local community college expresses his disappointment with the standards at McKinley:

> AS: Well, what's the caliber of student like? How does this school compare to other schools you've been to?
> M: Um, I don't think that the caliber of student is as high as I would like it to be. It's a, to me, it's kinda bad. For a lot of people it's a fall back school. If they don't get in somewhere else, if they don't get into State University, then they come here. And that's my perception. That for a lot of people, this is an alternative choice. It's not a first choice.

Here Michael not only offers his less-than-favorable impression of McKinley and his peers, but he does so through the commonly used comparison to State University. Not unlike Rachel and Ava above, as well as other participants within the study, Michael inadvertently positions McKinley as inferior to State University. In the same vein, Michael further discusses McKinley under a comparative lens:

> AS: When you were a high school student and you imagined what college was like, does McKinley fit that image?
> M: Actually, I found college a lot easier than I expected to. I figured when people go to college that they would be studying and seeking to do well and things like that and then I actually got to college, and like I said, I went to community college first and I was "ok, these are community college students" and I came here and it was the same kind of thing. A "C" was ok and before I started college at all, I always imagined college to be the top scholars, scholarly, and I was totally wrong. I don't think most people care here. I actually had more people that seemed more driven at community college than here, which is kind of unfortunate considering it's a four-year school.

Michael's comparison is reminiscent of the larger discourse surrounding community colleges. Like McKinley, these two-year institutions have a reputation as lacking academic rigor and the promise of educational opportunity (Brint & Karabel, 1989; Dougherty, 1994). They are also similarly composed of a majority of first-generation students from lower-income backgrounds. On the one hand, community college advocates maintain that these schools "are the most effective democratizing agent in higher education" (Dougherty, p. 6). On the other hand, it is argued that community colleges fail "to deliver the educational and occupational opportunity it promises" (p. 6). It should also be noted that, more recently, there has been a drop in the number of two-year graduates who transfer to four-year schools, "causing some to call two-year institutions dumping grounds for poor students" (Mullen, 2010, p. 8).

Interestingly, Michael positions McKinley and its students as inferior to two-year schools, which, as he implies, are inferior to four-year schools. Throughout interviews, McKinley was often compared to two-year institutions or as an extension of high school, followed by sentiments regarding academic rigor. Robert, a first-year student, majoring in Sociology, considers the intellectual climate on campus:

> AS: How would you describe the climate here?
> R: It's like thirteenth-grade business, still in high school but you're away from home and everything like that, and you feel like you're free to party.
> AS: What about on an academic level?
> R: It's not good. Most of the people that I know are on academic probation. Honestly, it's weird because I did nothing my first semester and got nothing but bs (bullshit); I don't know how they pull it off, but it's not good.
> AS: Do you feel that you're being prepared for the successful completion of your degree? I know you're only in your first year . . .
> R: I already skipped most of my general education classes so I've been taking lots of my majors and those are really interesting; I love those classes. But then with some of my general education stuff, they're awful. Like honestly, they make us take some classes that are just to hand us something . . . (inaudible) . . . It's like that Liberal Arts 101[3] . . . What I see them doing is getting us an education so we can get an education not for like anything. It has no substance . . . Basically you're getting nothing that has substance behind it where basically you know, you really learn about something where you actually know about your field. It's just—having you get a diploma to get a diploma and get into the workforce.

Robert, not unlike other students interviewed, felt disappointed with his academic experience at McKinley. His statements conjure an image of McKinley as an institution of higher education that produces an occupational discourse within higher education, one that is often associated with a working class ethos: "get a diploma and get into the workforce." This, of course, ignores opportunities for graduate education and the potential for higher-status, and often higher-paying jobs (those that position individuals to hold a certain degree of power). When Robert mentions that the school is *"just about having you get a diploma,"* we might interpret this to mean that there is something missing—that McKinley is failing to meet the "true" goal of higher education. Like most McKinley student participants, he is conscious of his location and feels disappointed by what he seems to believe is a second rate education. McKinley, for Robert, as well as other student participants, seems to serve as merely a credential dispensing institution. Faculty participants also identified a feeling of pushing students through to graduate for the sake of issuing diplomas. Amelia, an adjunct instructor in the art history program, also articulates the institution as one that is credential-dispensing rather than one that promotes practices that enable students to think critically, gain an appreciation for learning, and further their education beyond McKinley.

> AS: So what's your general sense of McKinley College? Academically?
> A: I think that there is a sense of getting them through the system, which is a little unfortunate. If somebody's having difficulty, not so much finding the root of the problem, but what can we do to mend it until it's not our problem anymore. So, I think because there's so many students here that it's not necessarily something that they can help on that level, but I feel like there's a lot of "just push them through" going on here.

As a less-selective, "credential-dispensing institution," McKinley suffers from a reputation of inferiority within the larger system of higher education, particularly as its identity is maintained in relation to State University and local two-year colleges. Institutional inferiority implies the intellectual inferiority of its students and other associated persons (Hollingsworth & Archer, 2009). McKinley's reputation as a substandard, working-class institution of higher education parallels and is reinforced by the history of the working class as such (Reay, 2001; Skeggs, 1997; Whitty, 2001). The "endurance" of McKinley's rusted institutional reputation extends into an image of the associated bodies moving within the institutional frame. This reputation stays and holds as part of public discourse, reinforcing a "discourse of injured identities." Inequity follows closely behind.

EMBODYING INSTITUTIONAL REPUTATION: A DISCOURSE OF INJURED IDENTITIES

It has been contested that social institutions are not merely external to human actors, but rather, institutions are internalized, and cannot be discussed separately from the human lives that move about within them. This line of thinking breaks with the more historical, but commonly held, sociological distinction between macro and micro analysis, which seems useful for a discussion of institutional reputation as one that becomes internalized and embodied.

Given the existing reputation of McKinley, one kept alive within the parameters of circulating discursive practice (which includes the rhetoric at the surface of social process and ideology, e.g. democratization, meritocracy), and following the logic outlined above, actors within and associated with the institution both influence, and are influenced by, the institution's working class habitus. McKinley arguably becomes classed by its reputation not only because a large percentage of its students do indeed come from working class and lower-income backgrounds, but because of the larger reputation of all public, urban institutions (which again, tend to be supported by the larger historical discourses surrounding the working class within the academy and reinforced by discourses surrounding rankings and quality). The reputation of McKinley (and that of the working class in education) permeates associated bodies, eventually working its way into the discourses of students, faculty, staff, and administration.

The discourse on campus reflects the larger Discourse surrounding institutional and working class reputation.[4] Mixing in the air and intermingling as tightly interconnected sounds, larger discourses turn to smaller discourses of injured identities. This becomes visible in observations and interview data of faculty, administration, museum staff, and students themselves, suggesting students on this campus are perceived to be broken and wounded by their *often assumed* and enacted "difficult," working-class lives—students who are limited and burdened by their biographical positions, ill-prepared to take on higher education, unless, as one faculty member mentioned, "within an institution such as this." These articulations hold heavy implications for students, faculty, and administration in terms of standards, expectations, campus culture, and future aspirations, as well as further educational opportunities. An instructor of art education and curator at the McKinley Museum of Art responds to my question regarding the "typical McKinley College student":

> Let me talk about the undergrads a little bit. They are not seasoned in the world. They're not out there to see, let's say, the arts or even music in a different way that will fulfill their lives as a life-long learner. They're struggling. They're struggling even maybe because of the money, because maybe they didn't have the education they needed, or maybe because they just don't have the IQ in the way that school was prepping them for college.

A faculty member of Social Work reinforces this discourse of injured identities:

> I think most have gone through a lot of hardship or they've had a hard time in high school. So when they get here, they're anticipating that this is just going to be a continuation of high school and get shocked but they're not sure how to do well. I think they come here lacking a lot of foundations that a lot of other colleges might already have and get upset when faculty will mark them down for not doing something when they never learned it in the first place.

Another faculty member claims:

> So one of the things we're trying to do is to change what they're thinking about, what the student's attitude is about education, which we feel we have to do in order to actually have meaningful higher education. They come from high schools with what I call the "every child left behind act" where their

teachers are told, "teach for the test or get fired." And so they're looking for things like a list of things to memorize for the next test, which they can then forget, and they do so with alacrity.

Students at McKinley are considered psychologically injured by academic inexperience, ill-preparation, cultural poverty, and general urban or rural deficit ("they are not seasoned in the world"). McKinley students are considered injured and intellectually, as well as culturally, weak simply because of their current positions at McKinley College and within the larger system. This discourse is clearly one of deficit, and whether student experiences and backgrounds are real or imagined, a damaging discourse is also reflected in the expectations and standards imposed by faculty and administration. Reflecting upon field notes, I am reminded of a rather discouraging conversation. Following the recording of an interview, Amelia, an adjunct instructor of Art History 101, a survey class offered as a general elective,[5] alerts me to faculty expectations and standards for students at McKinley:

> Immediately after releasing my record button, it was revealed to me that following her first semester teaching, her evaluations expressed distaste for the types of exams she had given. Prior to her second semester teaching art history 101, she was instructed by her department to change her format to multiple-choice exams. She was told that her standards were too high and her exams too difficult because "students here can't handle that format."

Art history, like all disciplines, requires more than memorization and rote learning—the level of thinking required of most American high school students—but demands conceptual, hypothetical, and judgment-based critical analysis. To suggest that students at McKinley "can't handle" anything beyond rote learning and multiple choice exams is to suggest that they are actually incapable of thinking on a collegiate level. Students who are believed to be incapable of thinking are not encouraged to do so, and unless students push beyond these invisible boundaries to their learning, they hit a "class ceiling" in higher education. In this example, discourse indeed becomes a damaging practice. Kate, a full-time professor of social work, reiterates common sentiments of her colleagues' feelings toward students at McKinley:

> I've heard a lot of professors say they're stupid so don't go that way. I mean, don't even do it. Don't even bother. That's what I was told when I started here. I said I was going to integrate some research into my teaching. [Other faculty said] Why bother doing that? They don't care or they're too dumb to get it.

These harsh expressions undoubtedly reflect a damaging discourse circulating among particular faculty, but the *affect* is far-reaching. Frank, an instructor responsible for the development of Liberal Arts 101, articulates faculty culture:

> The faculty culture is . . . I think faculty ultimately signed on for the right reasons but that doesn't last. They get socialized into the only possible reason that anyone would want to support the public, would want to support society, would want to support higher education is so that students can get jobs and that . . . and so they ignore that notion that this is something of value in and of itself. And society might support this just because it's something that society values and that people value and that . . . and so they're very reluctant to say . . . to be explicit about that, so very often you get people saying, faculty are talking about this, they don't see why we should have any general education at all . . . students should just come in and do their major and that's what college should be.

It is no surprise then that students are perceived as incapable and in a hurry to graduate. It is, after all, part of the nonverbal institutional message, or rather, the "expressive order of institutions" (embodied cultural/academic capital). As part of this expressive order, low expectations and mis/perceptions become embodied by students and faculty. Again, I turn to Amelia who expresses her impression of the "typical McKinley student":

> I think a typical one is kind of someone who has an agenda. They know what they need to get through and unfortunately, it seems to be "whatever I need to get there, the minimum is what I'm going to do." And it takes special students to go much deeper than that. I mean, the average staff has over 200 students and you have office hours two days a week. To have the average [number of students who come to office hours] be a person a week, that shows you that, despite your availability, unless there is an exam coming up and all of the sudden they're flooding in, but other than that, there isn't really a want to open themselves up to it much.

Amelia, in particular, struck me as an exceptionally fair, thoughtful instructor. In addition to talking at length during our scheduled interview, I also observed several of her introductory art history classes. I witnessed her try to persuade an enormous lecture hall of students to open themselves up to the material, to learning, and to succeeding academically, but Amelia too seemed to eventually leave some of her expectations at the door. Student participants' perceptions of one another, as well as faculty perceptions of students, communicate the larger Discourse of the institution and that of the working class within higher education, one that marks McKinley students as intellectually inferior to students positioned within colleges and universities of higher rank and reputation. This perception of students becomes threatening when it circulates widely and spreads into all corners of the campus.

As some professors become socialized into a faculty culture that seems to mark McKinley students as lacking, and as a result, lower standards and expectations, students internalize these messages, which also happen to parallel larger messages about the school itself and their (expected) place within higher education. Michele Tokarczyk (2004) writes of faculty working within less prestigious institutions (e.g., state and less prestigious private schools) "who resent their institutions' lack of prestige [and] shift their resentment to their students" (p. 162). For these faculty, "[r]ather than teach students the rules of the game—the study habits necessary for success—exasperated faculty sometimes dumb down their courses" (p. 163). The power of this damaging discourse takes hold, naturalizing reputation as a marker of identity, and in this case, as one marred by injury, inability, and intellectual inferiority. These imagined social facts of and surrounding McKinley College contribute to the endurance of its reputation.

DECONSTRUCTING MCKINLEY'S WORKING CLASS REPUTATION: IMAGINED SOCIAL FACTS AND THE POWER OF LEGITIMATION

Once the discourse surrounding reputation gathers speed and spreads, it turns into a naturalized account of reality and constitutes a form of social facticity "within a taken-for-granted system of norms, values, beliefs, and definitions" (Johnson, Dowd, & Ridgeway, 2006, p. 57). Reputation as social fact binds the institutional image to social consciousness and soon becomes taken-for-granted knowledge. These, now "imagined," social facts (e.g. all students at McKinley College are ill-prepared and intellectually inferior, working-class students are more interested in and better suited to vocational education) endure over time, despite challenges to these constructions of students from working-class backgrounds, as well as larger social, economic, and political shifts that ultimately permeate an institutional level, causing corresponding institutional shifts. Social realities, whether fully imagined or based upon facts, function in the everyday as unquestioned, objective realities. As Berger and Luckman (2002) explain:

> This means that institutions that have now been crystallized . . . are experienced as existing over and beyond the individuals who 'happen to' embody them at the moment. In other words, the institutions are now experienced as possessing a reality of their own, a reality that confronts the individual as an external and coercive fact. (Berger & Luckman, 2002, p. 45)

Not unlike the reputation of the working class in higher education, the reputation of McKinley College, as grounded in historical "fact" and popular images, has indeed become crystallized as a grossly limiting working-class social reality. Berger and Luckman (2002) assert: "This history itself, as the tradition of the existing institutions, has the character of objectivity. The individual's biography is apprehended as an episode located within the objective history of the society" (p. 46). The history of perceptions of the working-class in higher education has staying power, and the reputation of McKinley as a "working-class" institution characterizes and is embodied by its students. Over time, the inferiority associated with the working class in higher education, and McKinley's reputation as working-class, influence and produce larger socially constructed realities. McKinley's constructed reality suggests that standards are "naturally" lower and the educational aspirations of its students "naturally" end upon graduation. These beliefs, actions, and outcomes are reinforced, or legitimized, through meritocratic ideology and other seemingly "natural" processes or realities. As Johnson et al. (2006) make clear: "Legitimacy is a problem in the construction of social reality" (p. 57).

In light of the economic and societal-level changes that have shaped the system of higher education, American colleges and universities have been experiencing ongoing "academic drift" (Morphew & Huisman, 2002)—the process of modeling the structures and honoring the values of historically prestigious institutions to boost institutional rank. Rankings, however, provide their own set of imagined social facts. Ranking systems have been criticized as weak and unreliable measures of the quality of higher education (Brooks, 2005). In fact, for some, much of the news about university rankings has been deemed "meaningless noise" (Dichev, 2001). Rankings tend to convince many of the quality of education, but are often "designed by commercial media, driven by profit motives, and targeted to prospective students and parents" (Brooks, 2005, p. 1). Reputation, an influential feature of rankings (reputation influences rankings and rankings influence reputation), has become one of the more weighty measures (particularly within *U.S. News and World Report*) and determinants of institutional quality. However, many have acknowledged that this measure, in particular, "is based upon responses by those who may have a vested interest in the outcome" (Volkwein & Sweitzer, 2006, p. 131). As Malcolm Gladwell (2011) claims, "[w]ho comes out on top, in any raking system, is really about who is doing the ranking" (p. 75). In other words, there is a great deal of room for improvement in the underlying criteria for measurement, and there are a number of reasons for skepticism. For example, and of particular importance herein, reputational assessments are of the most heavily criticized. Many "[c]ritics have contended that they are no more than 'hearsay,' 'gossip,' or 'popularity contests' (Cartter, 1966; Dolan, 1976). . . . In addition, reputations reportedly have a 'staying' power that outlasts changes in the people or the programs (Cartter, 1966; Jones, Lindzey, & Coggeshall, 1982; Webster, 1981)" (Brooks, 2005, p. 7).

Rankings, like reputation, demonstrate that facts are not as *factual* as they seem, but are instead socially constructed, largely accepted measures of value and quality. These imagined social facts perpetuate social reproduction and inequality within education through their objectification and legitimation. But rankings, whether 'real' or imagined or assumed to be true, do tell us that schools are far from being equal within the field of higher education, and are instead, fiercely competing to maintain their positions. Competition is only able to take shape when held in relation to other entities, and only then do distinctions materialize and capital become realized. At the lower end of both ranking and reputation-based hierarchies, Mckinley sits and waits, though not without making its own attempts toward upward mobility. In response to social shift and competition within the system, McKinley's selectivity is on the rise, closing out more and more students from working class backgrounds and accepting more competitive students from middle class backgrounds (who now have more difficulty getting into more prestigious institutions and who reluctantly attend McKinley as a fall-back school). As McKinley's admissions statistics reflect higher criteria for, and lower percentages of, acceptance (the Office of Institutional Research indicate an increase in selectivity from 2006 to date), it becomes clear that changes are underway. These changes, however, appear to clash with the school's perceived working-class ethos and reputation (thus, the expressed reluctance for some middle-class students to attend McKinley). However, even as selectivity increases, the "best" students want to attend the "best" institutions, and the "best" students are less likely to choose a "working-class" institution. Suffice it to say, the endurance of reputation maintains a steady pace, and though not necessarily forever fixed to its subject, it can be carried intact through time, unmarred by change.

During an uncertain time of institutional transformation and economic shift, one thing is certain: social stratification remains deeply entrenched as a defining part of the system of higher education and reputation plays a large part in solidifying hierarchy. The larger Discourse of higher education, one that continues to ensure equality of opportunity, further solidifies the imagined social facticity of rank and reputation. Stanley Aronowitz (2004) best summarizes the "reality" of the situation:

> In reality, only about a quarter of people of working-class origin attain professional, technical, and managerial careers through the credentialing system . . . Typically graduating from third-tier, non-research colleges and universities, they have not acquired knowledge connected with substantial intellectual work: theory, extensive writing, and independent research. Students leaving

these institutions find jobs as line supervisors, computer technicians, teachers, nurses, social workers, and other niches in the social service professions. (p. 17)

Undergirding the development and maintenance of reputation, legitimating ideologies justify and reinforce systemic inequality. These legitimating practices help to affirm educational inequality within the institution itself. A Weberian conception of legitimation suggests that "even though individuals may not always hold the same norms, values, and beliefs, their behavior nevertheless becomes oriented to an order that is in accord with the rules or beliefs that they presume are accepted by most others" (Johnson, Dowd, & Ridgeway, 2006, p. 55). This construction of social reality becomes part of dominant discourse—a powerful part indeed. And "[b]ecause individuals perceive that others support this social order, the order seems like a valid, objective social fact" (Johnson, Dowd, & Ridgeway, 2006, p. 55).

CONCLUDING THOUGHTS

Beverley Skeggs (2004) writes that "[c]ontemporary representations of the working classes across political rhetoric, academic representations and popular media have nothing to do with the working classes themselves. Rather, they are about 'the middle classes creating value for themselves in a myriad of ways through distance, denigration and disgust" (p. 118). Skeggs points to an important relational quality. This is a quality that is indeed reflected in reputation as the working class is often deemed inferior when compared to the middle class. The reputational *affects* of this relationship are the embodied damaging discursive practices, words and utterances that structure reputation, and on a greater level, social inequality.

As a result of classed reputation, the following chapter argues that knowledge itself becomes classed, and curriculum, differentiated. Literature tells us that schools like McKinley with lackluster reputations (those at the bottom of the hierarchy) promote the practical application of knowledge as training for the workforce, while schools with elite reputations promote the pursuit of knowledge for its own sake. These classifications, which also correspond with class-based distinctions between mental and manual labor, provide seemingly natural distinctions and seemingly natural orientations toward knowledge.

NOTES

1. "Status Woods" is a pseudonym used to describe a suburb of the city in which McKinley is located. According to 2000 Census data, more than half of the Status Woods population is 98.65 percent White, 1.38 percent is Asian, 0.16 percent are Native American, 0.15 percent are African American, 0.04 percent are Pacific Islander, 0.19 percent are from other races, and 0.56 percent are from two or more races. Census data also indicate that the household median income was $68,003, more than double that of Arkive's.

2. Statistics, as presented here, are limited by the number of students who actually complete federal aid forms. In other words, these numbers may in fact be higher than they suggest. In addition, and perhaps more importantly, it is difficult to directly compare the percentage of first-generation students on these campuses. For example, State University has a much larger percentage of students coming from areas outside of the US. This alone complicates comparative institutional statistics.

3. Liberal Arts 101 is a pseudonym given to a course that is mandatory for all incoming first-year students. The course aims to teach students the meaning and importance of a liberal arts education.

4. Gee (2005) distinguishes between lowercase "d" discourse and capital "D" discourse. Capital D Discourse involves dominant Discourses (e.g. those expressed by institutions) and lowercase d discourse involves those expressed by individuals.

5. Art History 101 is offered as a general elective course. Typically, this course is made up of non-art history majors and is a more general cross section of the larger student body.

Chapter Four

*Clas*sifying Knowledge by Hand, by Head

> How interesting it is though, that our testaments to physical work are so often
> focused on the values such work exhibits rather than on the thought it requires.
> It is a subtle but pervasive omission. Yet there is a mind at work in dignity, and
> values are intimately related to thought and action. It is as though in our
> cultural iconography we are given the muscled arm, sleeve rolled tight against
> biceps, but no thought bright behind the eye, no image that links hand and
> brain.
> —Mike Rose, 2004, p. xv

Knowledge is neither of equal social value, merit, nor form; nor is it dispensed within institutions in equal measure. Knowledge is rather, much like
the social system itself, differentiated and classed. Since Durkheim's (1995)
strict dichotomizing of sacred versus profane knowledge and Bernstein's
(1977) more complex conception of opposing forms of knowledge (that
which is esoteric versus that which is mundane), the distinctions between
everyday, practical knowledge and academic or theoretical knowledge, have
become the foundation for what Derek Bok (2006) refers to as the "lamentable chasm" between manual and mental labor—a labor of head versus
hand. Long since mental and manual distinctions were formed, knowledge
requiring more practical application or skill has been designated to the working classes. The anti-intellectualism and physical brawn of the shop floor
Paul Willis describes in *Learning to Labor* (1977) applies to a long history of
the kind of intensive, corporeal, callous-producing labor associated with the
US and British working classes—the labor of the body. Indeed, when labor is
discussed, it is typically in reference to manual labor, and manual labor,
isolated from mental labor, has always been, and continues to be, the lower-
paying work of the lower classes. In this way, knowledge is clearly marked

and demarcated within and by the class structure, reproducing the differences between mental and manual types of labor while simultaneously building a hierarchical structure of knowledge.

In seeking to revive the old agenda of the "new" sociology of education—one that challenged the content and form of knowledge itself as contributing to social reproduction (Weis, McCarthy, & Dimitriadis, 2006), this chapter demonstrates how the constructions of social realities, in this case the constructed reality of McKinley College's working-class reputation, shapes the structure and content of knowledge. Moving further inside of reputation as a conceptual tool to investigate knowledge differentiation, this chapter examines the institutional messages communicated through various college documents and the ways in which these messages are carried through internal, representational voices, shaping pedagogy, curricular divisions, student attitudes, and campus culture.

Among a number of class-based bifurcations (e.g., blue versus white collar) the manual-mental division pervades higher education and bifurcates knowledge into competing discourses that firmly situate the vocational against the academic.

COMPETING DISCOURSES OF KNOWLEDGE

Interestingly, and contrary to popular belief, vocational education is not a thing of the recent past but a fixture of the deep history of American education. With the rise of industrialization, the nineteenth century historically aligned the practical and vocational with the liberal arts, as opposed to its more recent treatment within the academy as an increasingly isolated, separated, and undervalued tenant of higher education. In order to "preserve respect for the value of labor and for traditional notions of the work ethic, a moral outcome" (Rose, 2004, p.170) this period allowed for applied knowledge to be part of the discourse of liberal education. Earlier conceptions of vocational knowledge were, in this way, surrounded by and integrated into the discourse of the traditional liberal arts education. As Derek Bok (2006) reminds us, "In the words of Christopher Jencks and David Riesman, 'the question has always been *how* an institution mixed the academic with the vocational, not *whether* it did so'" (p. 26). However, somewhere along the length of history, a significant turn twisted this notion, pushing vocational knowledge into isolation, away from the "sanctity" of liberal arts education, and espousing levels of distaste (often intensely high) for vocational education from within the academy.

Many scholars identify this turn as having emerged following WWII, in the midst of a rapidly expanding system of higher education wherein increasing numbers of students from increasingly diverse backgrounds were enrolling in higher education. Institutional efforts to increase admissions often required schools to increase their vocational offerings and rethink students' primary concern: future employment. In doing so, curricula became increasingly divided and the "unity of knowledge . . . [became] an elusive ideal" (Bok, p. 25). Across colleges and universities, "a lamentable chasm separates the liberal arts college and professional departments" (Bok, 2006, p. 283). This chasm continues to widen across American colleges and universities, and becomes particularly damaging when we consider the differentiation of knowledge both *within* and *between* schools. Interestingly, the liberal arts, though argued by many to be rapidly declining in importance within the larger system, remain part of the highly valued structure and discourse of knowledge within elite colleges and universities, wherein critics of vocational education abound. Those contemporary critics of vocational education, many of whom could be charged with romanticizing higher education's past, are indeed greatly opposed to the growth and inclusion of vocational education for its lack of intellectual depth and perceived threat to the traditional liberal arts model. As Bok (2006) explains:

> Oddly, critics rarely . . . even pause to explain just why it is wrong for colleges to offer vocational programs; the very mention of the term vocational is considered enough to demonstrate the unworthiness of the offending institutions. Such disdain has its roots in nineteenth-century England, at a time when influential writers, such as Cardinal Newman, championed a liberal education free of any practical vocational instruction, and the young gentlemen attending Oxford and Cambridge were not supposed to "go into trade." (Bok, 2006, p. 27)

With the sustained growth and necessity of vocational majors as an external impetus, the discourse of higher education has shifted from one that was once liberal arts-centered, while often acknowledging the importance of and relationship to practical/applied forms of knowledge,[1] to a dichotomous discourse in which a liberal arts education is discussed and imagined as separate from, and superior to, vocational knowledge. These two separate and classed discourses within higher education reinforce existing social demarcations. If one were to examine the various measures of institutional quality, the system itself tells us that institutions committed to a liberal arts education tend to be elite institutions with the "best" reputations, rankings, facilities, and faculty, and admit only the "best" students. In contradistinction, discourse circulating within less prestigious institutions is arguably that of vocational education (though a liberal arts discourse also exists because it must be acknowledged for particular institutions to survive)—one that adjoins with discourses surrounding the working class and intellectual inferiority. The proliferation of these competing educational discourses[2] shapes class-based distinctions, while clashing, dividing, and building a durable hierarchy of knowledge at all levels of education. Competing discourses sustain the hierarchical order of knowledge and increase differentiation both within and between institutions whose status, rank, prestige, and selectivity just happen to correspond with the type of knowledge produced and disseminated within them.

Some time has passed since Jean Anyon (1980) introduced research on the overt and covert ways in which knowledge becomes differentiated through the quality/intellectual depth of materials used and the ways in which material is taught—the production of "qualitatively different types of educational knowledge" (Anyon, 1980).[3] Anyon's study, conducted within five elementary schools, demonstrates that knowledge itself is socially stratified, even within a standardized elementary-level curriculum. Since Anyon's research on school knowledge, now more than 30 years later, differentiation between and among form and content and the distribution of content as a contributing part of the structure of power and inequality, continues, but has emerged within postsecondary contexts of education. With an increasingly stratified system of higher education, a corresponding hierarchical system of knowledge correspondingly grows, and does so under the auspices of access and democratization. The contemporary context, however, adds deceiving levels of complexity to the severity of these competing discourses.

THE COMPLEXITY OF THE CONTEMPORARY SURFACE OF EDUCATION

The growth of mass higher education since WWII has led to changes in the character of both liberal and vocational studies, and not merely to the expansion of the latter. The pronounced distinction between them—with elite higher education always taken to mean a form of liberal education, and mass higher education a form of vocational education—no longer obtains. There are many schools and programs, both undergraduate and graduate, which are very much oriented towards specialized training for careers in government or industry, and yet are carried on through a pattern of relations between students and teachers which is not much different from that which characterized the collegiate arrangements at Oxford or Cambridge. (Trow, 2005, pp. 10-11)

The contemporary system does not offer as clear a picture of competing discourses as they play out across the academy. An image of an American system of higher education wherein vocational education (now pre-professional programs) is taken up, not only in less prestigious institutions, but within elite institutions, cloaks the severity of this divide. Further complicating the contemporary context, this rift between vocational and academic knowledge is not only located between schools, but *within* schools. Not unlike other lower-ranking schools, McKinley prioritizes the practical application of knowledge as training for the workforce, but does so through the rhetoric of a liberal arts education. All the while, schools with elite reputations continue to prioritize knowledge for its own sake, but they too do so in conjunction with more practical types of knowledge as the economy continues to place emphasis upon career/professional training across institutions of higher education. As institutions, across tiers, have become sensitive to the needs and desires of potential students, it would appear that the system, overall, values more practical knowledge. However, a wide curricular spectrum running the distance of institutional rank—from a traditional liberal arts education found within elite institutions, to a mix of liberal arts and preprofessional programs typically found within the larger middle of the spectrum, to preprofessional/vocationally-based education within the least prestigious postsecondary institutions—(Mullen, 2010) masks the degree to which these discourses continue to compete and the degree to which knowledge is differentiated.

The language used to articulate the vocational/academic divide, though still intact, does not quite capture the complex character of the contemporary context. During the early stages of growth within the system of higher education, newer colleges and universities were introduced with an emphasis on vocational goals, but today, as all contemporary institutions, at both ends of the hierarchy of higher education, market practical and applied forms of knowledge, language fails to reflect the same level of discord. The blurring of this more defined distinction between types of knowledge within the system is of great importance to our understanding of inequality. As Donoghue predicts:

> Like American society as a whole, with its widening gap between haves and have-nots, America's universities will grow increasingly stratified. The elite, privileged universities and colleges (about 100 of them, according to Barron's and similar surveys) will continue to function much as they do today, championing the liberal arts and the humanities and educating the children of the elite and privileged for position of leadership in law, politics, science, medicine, the corporate sector, and, of course, their own exclusive brand of higher education. (p. 84)

It seems the traditional notion of a liberal arts education extends only as far as its traditional institutional origins. Though it has been argued that the arts and humanities (those subjects which comprise a liberal arts education) are in crisis (Bok, 2006), threatened by massification, fast capitalism, corporatization, and other features of contemporary society, the liberal arts retain their central role in educating the elite. An article in *The New York Times* (Feb. 24, 2009) notes the state of the humanities and liberal arts education as one that is fragile under more recent economic pressures; however:

> The humanities continue to thrive in elite liberal arts schools. But the divide between these private schools and others is widening. Some large state universities routinely turn away students who want to sign up for courses in the humanities, Francis C. Oakley, president emeritus and a professor of the history of ideas at Williams College, reported. At the University of Washington, for example, in recent years, as many as one-quarter of the students found they were unable to get into a humanities course. As money tightens, the humanities may increasingly return to being what they were at the beginning of the last century, when only a minuscule portion of the population attended college: namely, the province of the wealthy. (Cohen, 2009, p. 2)

Studies on choice of college major, whether within the liberal arts or not, also indicate class-based divisions within higher education, closely tied to the differentiation of knowledge. Goyette and Mullen (2006) study the correlation between social background and choice of Arts and Science (A&S) fields of study and find that students from higher SES backgrounds are more likely to choose A&S fields of study and are more likely to go to graduate school. Their most important finding reveals a "connection between less prestigious institutions and high proportions of occupational-professional degrees" (p. 173). The authors "find a particularly strong occupational emphasis in institutions enrolling high proportions of students with low-test scores and, by implication, from lower socioeconomic backgrounds" (Goyette & Mullen, 2006, p. 173). Goyette and Mullen also speculate that "perhaps A&S degrees previously stood on their own as markers of cultural capital; with credential inflation, these degrees now require a prestigious institution behind them" (p. 503). The authors' findings further support the inextricable connections between cultural capital gains, types of knowledge, and reputation. This holds true even as there is a "growing utilitarian approach to university (and it should be stated with considerable emphasis that this is not unique to working-class or first-generation students)" (Lehman, 2009, p. 148). In other words, a liberal arts education remains elite, whether or not practical and professional programs coincide.

COMPETING DISCOURSES *WITHIN* MCKINLEY

McKinley is classified and self-promoted as a college that offers a strong liberal arts curriculum. The undergraduate catalog stresses McKinley's focus on "academics, with an emphasis on applied, marketable skills grounded in a strong liberal arts education." Evidence of a strong liberal arts education seems to equate to the College's broad offerings as it promotes several "excellent comprehensive academic offerings." The programs highlighted, including the visual arts, design, metals and jewelry, education, urban planning, and forensic chemistry, do not necessarily denote the strength of a traditional liberal arts education, which "historically consisted of Latin, Greek, philosophy, history, and science and now typically includes the arts and humanities, social sciences, math, and natural and physical sciences" (Goyette & Mullen, 2006, p. 498).

But aside from curricular matters, what does it mean to *be* a liberal arts institution? And what does it mean for McKinley, in particular? Traditional notions continue to define the small liberal arts college of the popular imagination: insular, elite, white, and cerebral, a campus adorned with preppy, blazer-wearing, squeaky-clean-cut bookworms with leather-bound classics tucked under khaki-colored corduroy sleeves. This image might then be enlarged to include the aesthetics of the grounds upon which these students traverse—tree-lined, manicured lawns, and well-preserved historic architectures—the kind of flawless landscape whose clean lines can be easily replicated by a cartographer or made into a three-dimensional model. Aesthetics aside, we know life on the campuses of elite institutions is far from an image of perfection, but we also know these small liberal arts schools continue to provide a curricular ideal that is a direct extension of their elitist scholarly pasts. As part of this ideal, students attending elite liberal arts colleges were expected to postpone "occupational training until they entered a graduate school or took a . . . job" (Jencks & Riesman, 1968, p. 263).

By contrast, McKinley is perceived to be "working class" and "urban"—both loaded descriptors within the larger discourse of higher education. In addition to negative connotations associated with a working class status, the word "urban," commonly used by student participants to describe the school, may very well be synonymous with Black, poor, and uninterested in academics. Interestingly, the most invisible part of McKinley's student population, from a student perspective, is actually White (2009 enrollment statistics indicate that among undergraduates, 15 percent are African American and 75 percent are Caucasian), though many White students with whom I spoke insisted that McKinley not only "caters to" Black students, but is a predominantly Black campus. Though statistics do show greater racial and ethnic diversity as compared to other US campuses, McKinley is indeed a predominantly White campus. The image of McKinley as described by students in the previous chapter marks racially-charged distinctions of urban/Black and suburban/White—meanings that are also deeply suggestive of social class. Though Black students do attend McKinley in higher numbers than cited at other schools, these students are far from the majority, and are even farther from filling the campuses of highly ranked, elite colleges and universities

(Bowen & Bok, 2000). This perceived hyper-visibility of Black students on McKinley's campus illustrates the complexity of class-based discussions—discussions that must include race.[4]

Aesthetically, this "working class," "urban" institution contrasts with the socially elite setting of a traditional liberal arts education. An abundance of wealth is not always visible in its architectures, in its classrooms, in its landscape, or in its students. Student parking lots, many of which are located on the perimeter of the campus neighboring rows of low-income housing, are not lined with expensive vehicles. New or renovated dormitories do not bend generously over the charm of a prosperous landscape. By contrast, McKinley is a campus with grit, cracks, and bumps, and though beautiful as it stands, several structures are in need of repair or renovation (e.g. there were several student complaints regarding the condition of a particular dormitory).[5] Appearances aside, McKinley students arrive onto this "working class" campus with pre-determined, deficit-centered "working class" reputations that do not seem easily altered in the minds of faculty, administration, or their peers. Classed reputations, as argued in the previous chapter, shape academic discourse and institutional structures of knowledge. Though arguably vocational knowledge has a place within a liberal arts model of education, it remains separated and continues to engender forms and quantities of academic capital that are not as highly valued by dominant groups and institutions.[6]

As Goyette and Mullen (2006) suggest, "[t]hose advocating liberal learning envision the university as an idyllic setting in which students devote themselves to the pursuit of knowledge and intellectual growth, temporarily free from the material demands of life" (p. 498). But the "typical" student at McKinley is hardly "free from the material demands of life." Instead, many McKinley students work while struggling to afford higher education, one that does not always provide an equal return for the investment. Indeed, many of the students with whom I spoke juggle part-time or full-time jobs while attending school and consider future employment a constant concern and the driving force toward graduation. McKinley is certainly not an anomaly among post-secondary institutions. Most students struggle to afford the increasing cost of higher education. The majority of student participants "chose" McKinley because it was the only institution they could afford, though many will still leave with considerable debt and without the quantity and type of academic capital that will enable real social mobility.

In fact, upon entering McKinley, it is assumed that students will first need to be educated on the definition and meaning of a liberal arts education. McKinley College insists that all first-year students take a mandatory course designed to teach both the foundations and significance of a liberal arts education. This "need" alone and singular effort in remediation is quite telling. The course webpage briefly describes the purpose of the program:

The Foundations of the Liberal Arts Program at McKinley College promotes an understanding of the continuity of human history, the depth of inherited knowledge, the validity of diverse modes of inquiry, the value of artistic expression and the richness of our collective experience. The purpose of the Foundations of Liberal Arts Program is to develop the skills and habits of the mind required for a life of intellectual curiosity and civic engagement.

James, the director of the program, who also happens to be the director of the Honors program, further discusses the program and its goals:

AS: Can you talk a little bit more about the Foundations of Liberal Arts? What are the goals of the course?
J: I'll give you the mission statement . . .
AS: Great.
J: . . . rather than recite it. It is a liberal arts program. It's explicit about that. And the meaning of liberal arts can be found in the book that we use for our first year program, for our first year course. So we have a required first year course called Foundations of Liberal Arts. And the idea of liberal education is written on, but it is to give people the capacities to be a free person in every meaning of the word. So it's to participate in society. It's to grow as an individual, to lead the examined life, and so on. And some of the articles that . . . some of the articles that have formed that are in this book. We actually, when we did this, we read this article as one of the things that everyone read. The other one was a book by Martha Nussbaum called *Cultivating Humanity* and this kind of gets at it a little bit but this, we have students read this; it's a shorter piece. It's rather challenging for first semester students, but if you don't give students something to reach for, they'll never reach. So we re-defined all of the learning. For the first time at McKinley we made a definition of the areas solely dependent on learning outcomes, in fact, course content. In fact, the culture of the college had been pure turf and it was perfectly acceptable to make the argument, "we need this course in order to support our major," not, "we need this course because this is a good course or content is important for people to learn outside the major." So now people don't make that argument in public anymore. They may think it, but they don't make that in public. So that's a cultural change for the college and try to push that further. So we're trying to ratchet up the intellectual climate on campus.

The course, however, only in its second year during the collection of data, has faced both faculty and student resistance. As James mentioned, students had difficulty recognizing the purpose and importance of the course. James describes the program as one he hopes will "ratchet up the intellectual climate on campus" and will bring about needed cultural change. Following a conversation with James about his own (considerably elite) upbringing, he commented on students "not understanding" his perspective on learning. I asked James what he thought about these differences:

J: They see someone like me as being not just different, but different in particular ways and part of that translates into elite, some notion of elite, you know, that . . . I don't think that idea is particularly well formed with students so it's kind of a very vague feeling as opposed to something they would point the finger at in the bad sense elitist, or in the good sense something to be emulated. I think there's probably swirling around in that feeling a little bit of both of those but it's not well articulated. It's not well thought out because it's not something they concentrate on much. I suspect if they did, it would become more evident what those feelings were and they'd develop them more, but they don't. It's just not that big of a concern except when they walk into your office and they see all your books and they walked in, "Have you read all these books?" You get that kind of question and I say, "Well, I haven't read all of them cover to cover. I've read parts of almost all of them." And I actually had a student say, "What do you do for your life? Read?" Read, think, write; that's what I do. And that's the kind of thing I mean, it's this assumption that that can't be, that that isn't . . . that lack of awareness of it. And this probably hurts them, too. I mean, not in the sense of career or anything like that, but some in ways, a deeper way. My sense is that many of the students here don't pursue those interests because they, I wouldn't say they devalue them explicitly; they're not supported. They don't see support in that direction; they don't see it as something that's done. It's these underlying assumptions. It's on the level of habits or something.

It is believed students at McKinley *need* a course such as this to introduce them to what a liberal arts education actually is because they have a certain "lack of awareness" about what it means to read, think, and write. This professor, a fourth generation Ph.D., born into a family that embraced the liberal arts as part of everyday life, imagines that students are not aware of what it means to engage with literature, with art, to read, to think, or to write because they are not supported in these endeavors—in other words, they lack a certain kind of knowledge that this particular course is trying to introduce. Though this course is meant as a kind of introduction to and remediation in the liberal arts, the surrounding campus discourse and culture does not reinforce this knowledge; in fact, much of this kind of material (and the degree of thinking involved) is often considered too difficult. Students who are neither encouraged to read, think, nor to write on a particular level across classroom experiences, and students who are not provided with the encouragement, support, and opportunity to proceed to graduate school, where their thinking will be engaged on a deeper level, again, bump up against a "class ceiling" in higher education. Though McKinley is classified as a comprehensive, liberal-arts focused college, offering a liberal arts education to all students, as an institution, it continues to prioritize applied learning and vocational education under the breath of a liberal arts education. The discursive treatment of these competing forms of knowledge further distances their idealized union, strengthens their disjuncture, and hides the ways in which knowledge becomes classed.

Through the democratization of an elite liberal arts model of education, institutions of higher education that are centrally organized around career training, while still liberal arts focused, build competing discourses of knowledge within their own walls. Because some forms of knowledge are more highly valued than other forms, and a correlation exists between economic capital gains and cultural capital gains (Bourdieu, 1977), competing discourses of knowledge both push and pull at students as they are propelled forward into the workplace, while deterring many from entering graduate schools. Messages of the importance of practical and applied knowledge mingle with messages of the importance of the liberal arts, and though these types of knowledge may very well be better learned as unified and interconnected material, competing discourses, as well as the perceived absence of a liberal arts education at McKinley, suggest that they are still significantly separate and distinct. The persistence of competing discourses, however, is at times marked by subtle differences—subtleties of differentiation that demonstrate signs of increasing equality, while reinforcing the same unequal structure.

THE SUBTLETIES OF DIFFERENTIATION

The following excerpt from a publication on McKinley's direct economic and cultural impact illustrates an emphasis on the applied and practical aspects of learning:

> With an emphasis on applied learning in a diverse campus environment,
> McKinley prepares students for the future—as teachers, scientists, artists,
> business owners, and other professionals. Many graduates enter the work-
> force in high-demand fields and are immediately employed. Because a large
> percentage of our graduates remain in New York, McKinley College is a
> major contributor to the economic and social fabric of this region.

The nature of this excerpt, though not entirely explicit in its underlying message, is one that emphasizes a particular type of learning for a particular type of student. McKinley's undergraduate catalog claims its student population is among the most diverse of all state institutions, enrolling "significant proportions of nontraditional (adult), first-generation, and disadvantaged students with demonstrated potential." The type of learning and type of learner embedded within this text are differentiated from the majority of students attending more prestigious, elite institutions that continue to place an emphasis upon the liberal arts. The generalized "types" that come from similar backgrounds and previous educational experiences enter McKinley and leave with credentials and opportunities that are often limited to entering the work-force. Considering that the majority of undergraduate students (Chronicle of Higher Education, 2010) report that they pursued particular institutions of higher education to "get a good job," the outcome for the majority of McKin-ley students would appear to meet the goal of both institution and student; however, this perspective neglects a more subtle difference. Rather than preparing students for the opportunity to enter graduate school, as is the case in more prestigious institutions, four-year colleges such as McKinley move students through to graduation and into the world of work (though of course, not without agency). This is not to suggest that accumulating practical knowledge or entering the workforce upon graduation is of lesser value; however, this distinction severs students from opportunities to go on to grad-uate school and earn higher degrees—in short, opening up different avenues by way of acquiring particular kinds of academic capital.

The self-promoting excerpt above describes McKinley as an institution with an emphasis on "applied learning" and one that enables students to get jobs, an incredibly attractive venue for many individuals hoping to get a degree and the immediate paycheck that follows. As a "major contributor to the economic and social fabric of this region," one that is economically destitute and socially damaged, McKinley offers the community prospects for renewal and change, as many of its graduates are positioned for "immedi-ate" employment; however, rather than entering graduate schools to poten-tially secure higher positions and higher incomes, many McKinley students are employed in service-oriented jobs that have little or no relevance to their earned degree. For example, a recent (2009) publication produced by McKin-ley's Sociology Department lists the types of careers its graduates enter upon completion of their degrees. Some of these careers include case-worker, youth counselor, crisis service worker, administrative jobs in social service agencies, substitute teacher, and career development counselor. Others find work in bank call centers, coffee shops, sales, and event planning. Listed below these positions (and other very similar job placements) is a smaller list of destinations for students who have gone on to graduate school (positions that include teachers, nurses, school counselors, academic advisors, college instructors, and research assistants). These lists demonstrate positions that are considered to be "low- and mid-level service jobs that do not (always) pay a decent working-class wage" (Aronowitz, 2004, p. 30). All are neces-sary, respectable positions, but do these 'professional' occupations represent the outcome of genuine mobility (Aronowitz, 2004, p. 30)?[7]

In further considering subtleties of differentiation, institutional mission statements are a telling source. The mission statement of any college or university is, simply put, a compression of its purpose, goals, and direction.

Colleges, as argued by Morphew and Hartley (2006), use "these statements in an effort to communicate particular messages, likely to specific and multiple audiences" (p.467). The authors suggest that institutions of higher education use these statements as a way of communicating "their utility and willingness to serve in terms that are both normative and politically apt" (p. 468). Though perhaps often delivered in vague terms, missions differ quite significantly, even if under similarly vague terms. Consider McKinley College's mission statement:

> McKinley College is committed to the intellectual, personal, and professional growth of its students, faculty, and staff. The goal of the college is to inspire a lifelong passion for learning, and to empower a diverse population of students to succeed as citizens of a challenging world. Toward this goal, and in order to enhance the quality of life in (the city in which McKinley is located) and the larger community, the College is dedicated to excellence in teaching and scholarship, cultural enrichment, and service. McKinley College will be a nationally recognized leader in public higher education, known: for the intellectual and creative accomplishments of its faculty, staff, and students; as a caring academic environment where lives are transformed through education and each individual is valued; and as an institution that serves to improve our region, our nation, and our world, one student at a time.

For the sake of an acute comparison, now consider the mission of an elite liberal arts institution, one that, as former dean of Harvard claims, "portrays employability as antagonistic to the true purposes of a liberal education" (Lewis, 2006, p. 6):

> Harvard College adheres to the purposes for which the Charter of 1650 was granted: "The advancement of all good literature, arts, and sciences; the advancement and education of youth in all manner of good literature, arts, and sciences; and all other necessary provisions that may conduce to the education of the . . . youth of this country." In brief: Harvard strives to create knowledge, to open the minds of students to that knowledge, and to enable students to take best advantage of their educational opportunities.
> To these ends, the College encourages students to respect ideas and their free expression, and to rejoice in discovery and in critical thought; to pursue excellence in a spirit of productive cooperation; and to assume responsibility for the consequences of personal actions. Harvard seeks to identify and to remove restraints on students' full participation, so that individuals may explore their capabilities and interests and may develop their full intellectual and human potential. Education at Harvard should liberate students to explore, to create, to challenge, and to lead. The support the College provides to students is a foundation upon which self-reliance and habits of lifelong learning are built: Harvard expects that the scholarship and collegiality it fosters in its students will lead them in their later lives to advance knowledge, to promote understanding, and to serve society.

Analyses of these particular documents reveal several points of interest. First, McKinley states that it is "committed to the intellectual, personal, and professional growth of its students, faculty, and staff." Unlike Harvard, McKinley's definition of "intellectual growth" is far more vague. One might also argue that the use of the word "growth," rather than Harvard's use of "advancement," is telling. One may interpret the usage of 'advancement' in this context to imply intellectual and social promotion, whereas 'growth' leaves more room for improvement. According to research on institutional mission statements, elite colleges tend to address intellectual growth as the primary commitment of the institution. In addition, elite missions do not share the same stated commitment to the growth of their faculty—elite faculty are revered and prized for already having achieved the highest form of excellence. 'The goal of the college is to inspire a lifelong passion for learning,' however, learning itself, as is argued here, is stratified and differentiated. Not unlike other documents mentioned, the differentiation of knowledge becomes apparent, though again in subtle ways, through the mission of McKinley as compared to that of an elite liberal arts institution.

Morphew and Hartley's (2006) examination of mission statements across institutional type demonstrates subtle distinctions in the ways in which the language used to convey "service" or "civic duty" is used within private and public institutions. Missions of public institutions promote service to the community, while private missions "enable men and women of diverse backgrounds to engage and transform the world" (p. 466). Morphew and Hartley conclude: "Suffice it to say that what 'service' means in one context is clearly not what 'service' means in another" (p. 466). This qualitative difference exemplifies a reproductive turn *inside* higher education—the rhetoric surrounding access and the democratization of education differentiates rather than equalizes and diversifies. Because missions are discursive texts that "speak" to particular audiences, these documents reflect the "expressive order of institutions" (Reay, Crozier, & Clayton, 2009) and tell us something about the ways in which knowledge is differentiated and embodied across tiers in higher education.

TRACKING CLASSED KNOWLEDGE

A number of scholars have taken up tracking in secondary schools, but the system cannot track children through early education without also tracking them into higher education, where this process arguably continues. The tracking structure within such a diverse, differentiated, expansive US system of higher education does not suddenly dissolve as students pass through high school and into college. At the point of entry, the secondary structure has been embodied and is carried into higher education. If we begin with the history of American secondary education, we are confronted with a similar structure demarcated by particular types of knowledge, for particular types of students, from particular types of backgrounds.

> By examining the larger contexts of student learning (e.g., curriculum and academic tracks), more comprehensive analyses of schools that serve diverse students also have noted that student underachievement is often perpetuated by students' differential access to high status knowledge and a "smart curriculum" (Oakes, 1985). (Gutierrez, 1995, p. 26)

Tracking, as a conceptual approach to studying educational inequalities, made significant contributions to sociology of education and the ways in which we understand the mechanisms of social reproduction; however, the majority of tracking research has been conducted within the context of K-12 education (Arum & Shavit, 1994; Lucas, 1999; Oakes, 1985, 2005, 2008). Though "the old system of completely separate and explicit academic, general, and vocational programs, found in a few of the *Keeping Track* schools, has now largely disappeared," Oakes informs us that "most American schools are still keeping track" (2008, pp. 704-705). Research still finds curriculum between tracks to vary quite widely, and with so many more students entering higher education, these preceding tracks determine future opportunity structures (e.g. access to what?). In spite of increasing college admissions (as well as increasing graduate school admissions) and degree inflation within an increasingly stratified system of higher education, nearly all research on tracking ends upon high school graduation. As one of the few studies that looked at tracking within higher education, Alba and Lavin (1981) studied community colleges as a separate track within postsecondary education—the other track, of course, constituted by four-year institutions. The authors determine that "community colleges generally deter students from attaining their educational ambitions" (p. 223). Findings reveal these two-year, open-admissions colleges act as an extension of early-educational, non-academic tracks through curriculum differentiation and subtle institutional messages, which suggest students lack the ability to move on to four-year schools. Relevant to the argument herein, the authors find:

> The vocational programs influence the academic culture at these colleges and provide students who are being discouraged from pursuit of the baccalaureate with a substitutive goal, the associate degree in a vocational subject. (Alba & Lavin, 1981, p. 236)

Indeed it seems significant that 40 to 60 percent of community college students are enrolled in vocational education, or rather, in occupational-education programs (Dougherty, 1994) as opposed to programs that disseminate knowledge conducive to continuing one's education. This, combined with the significant decrease in the number of community-college transfers (to 4-year institutions), makes an interesting and significant case for tracking in higher education.

In addition to literature that argues that community colleges are (as a collective) a lower track within the system of higher education, this research illuminates an increasingly popular trend that corresponds with the growing stratification within the system of higher education—a trend that positions students within different tracks, not only *between* particular colleges and universities, but also *within* them.

THE HONORS PROGRAM: TRACKING ELITE KNOWLEDGE

In September 1996, Massachusetts Board of Higher Education member Aaron Spencer proposed to create an elite public college to attract honors students from around the state to the public higher education system (December 1996). A concept paper for "Commonwealth College" was circulated by the Board in December, advocating a college that would support 1500 to 2500 students, have tough admissions criteria, enforce a strict honor code, and require a thesis from all graduating seniors (Massachusetts Board of Higher Education 1996). (Bastedo & Gumport, 2003, p. 352)

Following the Massachusetts Board of Higher Education, the City University of New York (CUNY), among others, developed honors programs to improve enrollments. In doing so, CUNY honors students were ensured the best facilities, faculty and opportunities. According to Executive Vice Chancellor Louise Mirrer (CUNY Matters 2001), these students:

will be taught by a pool of the most talented, most creative faculty from our undergraduate, graduate, and professional schools if an upper division wants to study with, say, a scientist working on huge magnets at City College's Structural Biology Center, that could be done. If an Honors College student wants to study with a leading scholar anywhere in the University, we'll facilitate that. (cited in Bastedo & Gumport, 2003, p. 352)

If a traditional (elite) liberal arts education does exist at McKinley, it is offered to students enrolled in the Honors Program. Students accepted into the Honors Program are cordoned off from McKinley through their own academic and social communities—separate classes, separate residence halls, and a separate student-run publication, enable students to distance themselves, both symbolically and physically, from McKinley's non-honors students.

Established in 1984, the All College Honors Program currently enrolls more than 160 students. Those who enroll understand that although they are expected to work hard, they are rewarded with opportunities for applied internships, scholarships, research, and bright futures. All College Honors Program students engage in special seminars, receive individual attention from dedicated, highly qualified faculty members, are rewarded with scholarships and awards, and have access to their own residence hall and lounge.

To be admitted, honors students must have excellent records of academic performance. More specifically, "high school students must have a grade point average (GPA) of 90 or higher (or rank within the top 10 percent of their graduating class) and have SAT scores of 1100 or higher and/or ACT Composite of 24 or higher. Advanced Placement courses with grades of B or better, co-curricular activities, and community involvement also are considered" (Honors webpage). High school advanced placement courses, an academic track for the more privileged of students, immediately position potential students within the Honors Program. Honors at McKinley becomes an affordable, but privileged, option for academically strong students who may not get into their preferred schools or who are unable to afford other options. Hannah, an Honors senior at McKinley, discusses her experience:

AS: So, it sounds like you really loved McKinley?

H: Yeah, yeah, ever since day one I have been really involved. I know that when I am put in a place, an institution where my hand isn't being held, I am given a whole lot of information that I can take and run with. I pile way too much on my plate, first of all, then I had to learn how to do time management, but I work really well in a non-spoon-feeding environment. So when I got to McKinley, I had the honors program, which is like a private school within a public school.

AS: Can you tell me about that? How you think it is different?

H: The honors program? Well, it is . . . I love it and I am close with the director of the program. He is just an all around good guy. His classes are unique, they are not extra classes, but they make up the credits of your GEs (general ed.) and they take 3 of the 6 credits, so it covers like a social science, and then math and arts, but they are lectures and they are also hands-on and they have been having a regular faculty do it, but sometimes they switch it up if they find a new professor who wants to get involved in the honors program because they don't have to teach exactly what they teach in their regular classes. They can take what their specialty is and go off on it because they can take it to these students who are expecting to be challenged. This is why I like it and the classes are smaller, even if you are taking a general education class, it is like 30 kids. So that has been really awesome.

AS: Favorite classes?

H: I had this one, it is called values and ethics in the professions, but really it is the sciences versus the humanities . . . how they relate and how they differ and if these two cultures are really one? One of the professors would play off his role big time. He is a PhD in chemistry, conservative mind, and over here you

have the head of the writing program. She was definitely a hippie. Both bril-
liant people, so smart, but she would play the liberal and they would debate
and teach. They would throw it at us and we would have to talk about it, so
classes like that . . . really cool. And I didn't have other classes like that. I had
this conversation with a professor of mine because she put some questions up
on the board, that are universal questions in art history, but we are applying it
to what we were looking at (the slide). It was like me and two other people
maybe who were really into the conversation and discussing it, even if it is
wrong [their answers to questions] and afterwards, I had a great class, you
know, I loved it, and she was like "you know, was that detrimental to the rest
of the class?" I said I just don't think a lot of students have had enough of that
during their college education, maybe even their education in general, where
they feel comfortable to even try to discuss like that. If they don't have those
tools, how are they possibly going to have the confidence to try to say stuff in
class?

Hannah, like the other honors students with whom I spoke, presented deep
inconsistencies between the structure of classes, knowledge, and her peers
within the Honors Program and those within the larger campus. Consumption
and dissemination of knowledge then becomes differentiated within the same
campus. Though this research was not designed to locate honors students as
intentional participants or with an eye toward tracking, I inadvertently interviewed three honors students (including Hannah). Consistencies among these
three students, all of whom were art history majors, Caucasian, female, and
ostensibly middle class, captures a small piece of evidence of tracking within
McKinley College. It seems Oakes is right to suggest that most schools are
"still keeping track," but it also seems that this trend is finally moving into
the realm of higher education.

CONCLUDING THOUGHTS

This chapter argues that the long-established chasm between the liberal arts
and vocational education assembled and preserves a durable hierarchy of
knowledge.

Bourdieu argues that the differentiation of knowledge is legitimized by
the field itself through elite recognition and valuation of particular forms of
academic capital—capital embodied by institutions and internalized by individuals at the top of the educational hierarchy. Legitimate knowledge thus
becomes knowledge valued by more dominant groups. It becomes the most
socially and culturally "profitable" form of academic capital, but also more
easily appropriated by individuals who embody an elite habitus. But legiti-

mate knowledge also gives way to its relational binary, knowledge that is not as highly valued: the practical, vocational education associated with and demarcated to the working classes.

The following chapter further explores the embodiment of institutional working-class habitus—one that positions students within the field of higher education and aligns them with particular opportunity structures secured through the appropriation of particular kinds of academic capital. In using the visual arts as an example of democratized elite knowledge on McKinley's campus, the following explores language use and literacies as "discursive resources" (Hanks, 2005), or forms of capital, and as products of individual and institutional habitus that structure students' trajectories.

NOTES

1. As Derek Bok (2006) asserts: "Moreover, vocational courses are hardly new; they have been a fixture in American higher education since the Morrill Act of 1862 declared that the leading object of the new land grant universities would be, 'without excluding other scientific or classical studies, to teach such branches of learning as are related to agriculture and the mechanic arts'" (p. 26).

2. In *Degrees of inequality: Culture, class and gender in American higher education*, Ann Mullen (2010) refers to these discourses as the "competing narratives" of education.

3. Though Anyon's study of *Social class and school knowledge* (1980) suggests powerful reproductive implications, it is important to note that the author ends with non-reproductive possibilities of school knowledge.

4. While minding the importance of intersectionality, this research acknowledges that social class is but one social construction among many (e.g., race/ethnicity, gender) contributing to social stratification; however, it is through the lens of social class that stratification most clearly displays itself herein.

5. Though Yale is an example of a traditional, elite liberal arts institution, it is also situated in the absence of wealth relative to the surrounding neighborhoods, but unlike McKinley, the contrast of internal wealth (within the campus gates) and the surrounding environment is quite striking.

6. In the past, elite knowledge was simply that which was inaccessible to the "non-elite," whereas Paul DiMaggio's more recent work argues that the elite now must acquire high brow, middle-brow, and low-brow knowledge to *be* "elite."

7. Aronowitz mentions particular occupations that, in many cases, present social mobility for those of whom would not have otherwise climbed without the education and credentials necessary for the position (e.g. teachers). Nevertheless, Aronowitz forces us to rethink the opportunity structure of higher education.

Chapter Five

Elite Knowledge within a Non-Elite Context

Language, Literacy, and "Intertextual Habituality"

AS: Would you say McKinley places emphasis upon the arts?
Brad: Yeah, I mean 'cause they have a lot of galleries. I think this is an artistic campus. I mean especially when you walk around and see the structures, not the buildings but the art things like different shapes and stuff.
AS: Oh, the sculptures?
Brad: Yeah, the sculptures.
—Brad, fine arts student, McKinley College

The contrast between the title of this chapter and the quotation that immediately follows demonstrates a notable distinction between the use of language and levels of literacy. These two sets of expressions, removed from the context of an interview and juxtaposed here as an introduction, illustrate expressions of classed knowledge. According to Bourdieu, these expressions indicate individuals' mental and corporeal habits, dispositions, and perceptions—the embodied structures of social space. The distinctly different use of language indicates the education, literacy, and arguably the class, of its author—the title is an example of carefully constructed esoteric, elite (high status) knowledge—that which has been legitimized within the intellectual field. It is grossly intentional and jargon-laden and its obscurity becomes more visible as it sits uncomfortably above a more casual description of art, boldly emphasizing the privilege of its author. Just look at the divisive colon separating text and staging conformity—it delivers an academic punch of normality, of consistency with other books of its kind. And what is "intertextual habituality" anyway? All of this stands above the response from Brad, a community college transfer, fine arts major. His language and patterns of expression here appear quite different—the use of a more informal, everyday language to describe sculpture as an art "thing." Brad did not struggle to conjure up the "appropriate" term "sculpture," one that is arguably basic to an academically-inclined visual arts vocabulary, but relied instead upon the words "structures" and "shapes" to describe the abstract art forms placed throughout the campus of McKinley College.

Situated above Brad's casual description, the chapter title also assumes an authoritative role of producer and protector of legitimate knowledge as it frames and interprets the use of language located outside of academic discourse. Of course, identifying these distinctions only further lends to the power of legitimization. As a student at McKinley, Brad's placement within the system of higher education and the art world is decidedly a position at the lower end of the social hierarchy—his language is not of the dominant, high-status, or legitimized kind (Bourdieu, 1991; 1993; Hanks, 2005).

As part of a liberal arts education, the visual arts occupy an important space within higher education, and also one that is uniquely connected to historical and existing hierarchies of knowledge. Once no more than the exclusionary knowledge of the elite (not unlike higher education itself), the visual arts, through the process of democratization, is now argued to be among the shared, socially-inclusive knowledge of the general public. Alongside other related social processes (for example, marketization), the visual arts as "high culture" have transformed over time and moved out of the exclusionary context of the elite and into the realm of "popular culture" (Collins, 2002). This phenomenon (democratization) is not one that is singular or removed from the context of other 'fields,' but is interconnected and intricately tied to the field of higher education (Wallach, 2002). As a continuation of the past, the visual arts are directly disseminated within two primary contexts: university art history departments and art museums.[1] The lines of connectivity running between these sites reveal the history of two histories of art (Haxthausen, 1999), which will serve as the contexts for this particular chapter. Though relatively little has been written on this relationship between art museums and art history departments, one that arguably remains rather tenuous, it is a relationship that offers important insight into the complexity and construction of the hierarchy of knowledge within the homologous fields of higher education and the art world. Haxthausen (1999) recalls: "Joseph Alssop called art history and art collecting 'the Siamese Twins,' because art historians define the categories and establish the canon for the collector, and collecting is inevitably linked to commerce" (p. xv). Closely connected, the art museum and university art history departments share their own elite history within the field of cultural production and as producers of elite knowledge. Haxthausen (1999) further acknowledges the interconnectivity of this relationship: "Not only is the museum as much a site of art historical scholarship as the university, but the ostensible boundaries between museums, which by necessity must associate directly with the agents of power and commerce, and academics, who often assert their moral disdain for that world, are in fact false boundaries" (p. xiv). The rich histories and complex contemporary positions of institutions of higher education and the American art museum make the visual arts an interesting and unique form of knowledge, as it crosscuts two distinctly different, though homologous, fields.

Appropriately then, this chapter seeks to interrogate the visual arts, in particular, as a form of elite knowledge (dominate academic capital) within the "democratized," "non-elite," discursive space of McKinley College. While considering the interrelated analysis of the two previous chapters, this chapter begins within the social space of "working-class McKinley," gathering an empirical basis for the interwoven analysis of the relationship between habitus (both that of students and of the institution) and the proliferation of discursive formations surrounding the visual arts, again, as a form of elite knowledge. Following this more general vision of valuation of the arts on campus, the path of analysis moves into the sub-field of art history through the study of McKinley's art history program. Though restricted access to the Art History Program presented serious limitations, such as a shortage of interview data, it is believed that the accumulation of data from various sources, and through the use of various methods, allows for sufficient critical analysis and interpretation. The trajectory of this analysis then returns to the relational space of the McKinley Museum of Art, a culturally charged context involved in the preservation and distribution of elite knowledge.

THE PROLIFERATION OF A SINGULAR VISUAL DISCOURSE

> Schooling is not ideology-free, and language and language/literacy education is . . . the prime carrier of the dominant ideologies and cultural values in which school practices are consciously or unconsciously embedded. (Clark & Ivanic, 1997, p. 49)

Interviews across disciplines with students, faculty, and administration indicate that McKinley College, collectively speaking, does indeed value the arts. At the outset of my research, this was a question provoking the direction of study, but has since turned to the more appropriate question regarding *how* the arts are valued. Reception of the aesthetic realm of the visual arts is often conceived as having a dualistic differentiation, much like the description of knowledge discussed in the previous chapter. The visual arts, when divorced from the distinctly cognitive structures of knowledge (often discussed as "visual literacy," introduced by Debes in 1968) become part of a singular discourse that is expressed through the practical and applied elements of the arts. This discourse is often associated with a general understanding of art that becomes distanced and removed from the elite knowledge of the field.

At McKinley, discourse surrounding the valuation of the visual arts is primarily expressed through the appreciation for the hands-on practice of the production of artworks, but more importantly, a practice that is seemingly isolated from academic discourse. Students at McKinley College, as well as faculty perceptions of students' valuation, voice the proliferation of a singular, isolated discourse surrounding the visual arts. This singular discourse projects the valuation of arts contribution to the everyday, rather than for its own sake (as is modeled in the discourse of elite education). Singular discourse circulates as students discuss the ways they value the arts in terms of applied forms of knowledge, and though this is not an unusual way of discussing art appreciation, attention must be turned toward the *absence* of an elaborated discourse that includes the articulation of *intertextual* knowledge. As students "expand their visual repertoire of visual references," as well as references that are text-based, they also "extend the web of intertextual threads" (Tucker, 2002, p. 8) from which to pull, articulate, and formulate insight. In other words, intertextual (or elaborated) discourse allows for the accumulation, activation, and application of academic capital. "Habitual intertextuality," a concept introduced by Roz Ivanic (2004) is illustrative of the relationship between forms and levels of language use, literacy, and individual/class habitus. Ivanic, following Bourdieu's concept, describes a similar kind of embodiment: "As discoursal and generic resources become internalized from encounters with real people and real texts, they become part of a person's socially structured and structuring habitus" (pp. 286-287). If one follows Bourdieu, exposure to elite knowledge alone is not enough to instantiate the privilege accrued through habitus that is developed around the accumulation of an intertextual repertoire of highly valued (elite) texts and discourse.

Though little social research suggests curricular and knowledge differentiation within higher education, if we consider the context of elite boarding schools, we notice intense parallels between elite secondary curricular discourse and that of elite post-secondary. Rubén Gaztambide-Fernández (2009) writes: "Elite boarding schools continue to offer an extensive curriculum that often rivals that of small liberal arts colleges" (Gaztambide-Fernández, 2009, p. 28) and with these offerings, similar discursive treatment follows. Similarly, Shamus Khan's research (2008, 2011) demonstrates an elite private secondary discourse that inscribes in students a sense of breadth, depth, and integration of knowledge. Discussing the Humanities Program at St. Paul's, Khan remarks:

This program does not teach students to know "things." The emphasis is not on knowledge of historical happenings, for example. Instead it is on "habits of mind" that encourage curiosity and exchange. Integrating religion, art, philosophy, politics, history, and literature, the course presents students with a sense that there are "great questions" that unify a variety of academic disciplines. But the unifying impulse is not a dominating one. Students are also asked to "interact" different texts: literature, theology, movies and compose in a variety of forms. In short, the curriculum has a hedgehog-like unifying impulse ("great ideas") while insisting that students engage in fox-esque activities (comparing disparate texts). Most importantly, though, students are not taught things about the world. They are taught "habits" and how to "interact" things within it. (Khan, 2008, p. 198)

In this elite private school, students engage in classroom discussions that encourage the kind of relational thinking involved in intertextual discourse and become better equipped to take high-status positions, within high-status institutions, that will further increase their high-status academic capital. In Khan's description, "students read poetry, drama, and prose from both literary and historical perspectives, and they learn to recognize universal themes while making connections between ancient and modern texts, or between film, visual art, or music" (2008, p. 199). To "see" the visual arts in this way, allows students to build and cultivate elaborated discourses. Khan (2008) further illustrates:

The impact of Florentine Neo-Platonism in Renaissance culture is discussed, and the artists of the glorious High Renaissance—especially Raphael, da Vinci, and Michelangelo—are analyzed with an eye towards their compositional structure as well as content. The focus then shifts to the Protestant Reformation and its impact on Elizabethan England in general and Shakespeare's plays in particular—one of which is the culminating text of the term. (p. 202)

When an appreciation of practice (structure) is paired with the intellectual components of appreciation (content) and an understanding of intertextual relationships are established, value becomes recognized by art's dominant discourse. This discursive distinction (singular and elaborated discourse) is captured through context-specific deliberations of language use and language-in-use.

In the following excerpts, students respond to questions regarding the importance of art to their lives, leaving a space for each to narrate the ways in which art (in all forms) has influenced their lives and the ways in which value is articulated. Christine, a design major, describes how valuable the visual arts, in particular, are to her everyday life:

To me, because it's something that I've been so influenced by, it's kind of like everything. I just . . . I just moved into my apartment and I have all this artwork from my old school so I just finally had a place to put it all and finally got to put it on the wall and I come home almost every day and do something with my sketch book. I feel like I was lucky because it was encouraged, whereas I know a lot of students who weren't encouraged in the arts, and it's funny because growing up, it was something I was so into. I loved it . . . I had drawings . . . I was obsessed.

For Christine, art is "everything." From her description above, one would express little doubt that she values and appreciates the visual arts. Christine surrounds her own living space with drawings and artworks she made in former studio classes. For Christine, art is lived-in and part of her everyday existence. But Christine communicates this valuation through the act of making art and in the absence of an elaborated academic discourse. Though visual art physically surrounds Christine (both on and off campus and both externally and internally), its appreciation is articulated through its proximity (hanging within her personal space) and use. Christine is an example of other conversations with students, both in and outside of the arts, who expressed similar conceptions of value—through an affinity for the production and skill-based practice of the arts in the absence of discursive elaborations that suggest the appropriation of elite knowledge. Erica, a communications major, responds to the same question:

E: I like a variety of music, I always have. And just sometimes songs can be very inspirational and sometimes I just like the beat. And I do like that. Especially if I'm having a down day and there's a fun song on the radio, I'll be like "yeah" and especially, not to be mean, but they're bashing guys and it helps sometimes. It really does. So definitely everyday . . . I'm looking to music to help, especially when I'm at home. And sometimes, I just zone out from everything else. It helps me, like, get away. I like that.
AS: The arts in general?
E: Um, I can't really say. Can I get into architecture? I love seeing things like that. I've been begging my friends to go to art museums or just . . .
AS: Really?
E: I've been dying to go to the Museum of Glass . . . dying to go there.

Like other art forms, the art of glassblowing can be appreciated for the skill involved in addition to its aesthetic qualities; yet in the case of glassblowing, the form often has a function and is recognizable. This distinction becomes important as art is often, in popular discourse, associated with the conceptual and craft with production and function. The Museum of Glass, unlike many marketing campaigns of other art museums and galleries, emphasizes the hands-on nature of art from a "make your own glass souvenir" to daily glassmaking demonstrations. The art/craft distinction has long been determined by function and practicality—"craftworks must be functional, whereas fine art need not, even should not, have any practical use" (Boden, 2000, p. 289). Though more recent scholarship attempts to blur the line between art and craft (Boden, 2000), the status-bearing history of this distinguishing line resists distortion.

> The distinction between "art" and "craft" carries an accumulation of intellectu-
> al baggage, including a long history of philosophical controversy. It also bears,
> in our culture, a number of sociological differences. Practitioners of art and of
> craft tend to belong to distinct professional groups, whose activities differ in
> social status and economic reward. (Boden, 2000, p. 289)

Erica's response might also be read as another rather subtle distinction, but tells us something about the class-based structure of knowledge. Though she expresses a feeling of importance for the arts in her life, Erica mentions popular music on the radio as a form of art that brings her pleasure and helps her "to get away." Popular music, though indeed part of the art world, is held in contradistinction from the elite knowledge of the products of art's elite history, much like its institutions. And though the popular has spread into elite contexts as part of elite consumption, Erica's response to my question is articulated through the use of these more accessible art forms and institutions (e.g., guy-bashing songs on the radio and the Museum of Glass) in the ab-sence of academic intertextual, elaborated discourse. Matt, a first-year educa-tion major also articulates the value and importance of art to his life through its application:

> AS: How important or valuable are the arts to your everyday life?
> M: To my everyday life? I think they're pretty important. I'm not sure how . . .
> AS: Why would you say they are important?
> M: I'm extremely interested in art.
> AS: The visual arts?
> M: Visual Arts, and I play music as well. It's, I don't know. I do a lot of art
> myself. I do some painting, some woodcarving and stuff like that.

Matt's response to my question is a difficult one for him to articulate. He believes the arts are valuable, but isn't quite sure how. Matt, like Christine and Erica, discusses the ways in which art is valuable through its practice alone. It is also interesting to note that Matt uses the term "woodcarving," a term that, like Erica, denotes craft. The visual arts, for Matt, Christine, and Erica are a practice of skill, existing as both craft and hobby (drawing, painting, listening to music, or woodcarving). These students express the valuation of the arts through a language that is consistent with that of their institution. Students attending more elite institutions communicate valuation quite differently by referencing other artists or works of art and talking about the formal qualities of art that communicate an idea or expression. Even in discussing the practice of art, students with a larger vocabulary of images, texts, and history, are able to pull from a much larger net of "legitimate" knowledge to articulate meaning and value in conjunction with skill.

Despite not having background in or knowledge of the arts, Maya, an education major, discusses the importance of the arts to her life:

> AS: How important are the arts to your everyday life?
>
> M: Arts? It's pretty funny because I'm not an art person but thinking about art is like music is an art and I listen to all sorts of music and also, I do not know what is art. When I walk around McKinley, there is a fancy kind of art, I don't know who created it.
>
> AS: The sculptures?
>
> M: Yes, the sculpture. Sculptures are a kind of art, right?
>
> AS: Yes.
>
> M: It's kind of funny. To look at the sculptures and say to myself "why the hell did they put this thing in here?" "What does that stand for?" I would first look at one of the sculptures right in front of here and I'd say "oh my gosh, that sculpture is falling down." Also, when I go to some of the parks, there are naked sculptures around. And I was like "oh my gosh!" A guy . . . you can see his penis and all of that stuff. It embarrasses me, but I'm used to it now. Actually, there is more girl sculpture art than guy sculpture art. We were in a field trip . . . I do not know where. I do not remember . . . all these sculptures . . . all the girl sculptures, naked boobs and everything, all the guy's were saying "oh look at that" and I said "when will I get the chance to see a guy sculpture?" It was really funny.

The academic language Maya uses to describe sculptural works of art is considerably underdeveloped. Maya's higher education has not afforded her the language that demonstrates a depth of knowledge or higher levels of visual literacy, which would enable her to compete within the larger field of higher education, particularly as she does intend to go on to graduate school. Maya's higher educational experience may be introducing her to the visual arts through a certain level of exposure (sculpture as public art exhibited on campus, etc.), but does this provide the necessary academic capital to enable mobility?

Faculty participants often acknowledged the valuation of the visual arts for McKinley students while also acknowledging the class-based habitus of students as one that may clash with that of art institutions (like the McKinley Museum of Art and the International Museum of Art). Tom, a professor of history, who has taught at McKinley for nearly thirty years, discusses the importance of the arts for both faculty and students:

So it's intrinsic to the core curriculum of the college. Also, McKinley, one of its schools, it's called the School of Arts and Humanities and the arts are a big part of what attract students to McKinley. Although most of our students are working-class, or lower-middle class, a lot of them are attracted to the arts. A lot of them come from other states to study the arts here . . . fine arts and arts education and the like. So it's a big attraction here and it's a big part of the curriculum. There's a large student population in the area. I'm amused at the examples. Schools I've worked in the past, to get into ethnic stereotyping, schools I've worked in the past or as a visiting professor, would have large numbers of populations, usually immigrants, Asian countries, China, Thailand, you name it, and stereotypically, they'd be studying the exact sciences or engineering. When you see the Asian kid at McKinley, he or she is probably studying the arts. If they wanted to study engineering, they'll go to State University (laughter). State University also has a very fine program in the arts as well, I must say. Outstanding programs in the arts with first-rate people, but it's a big draw here. It's a long history, distinguished artists and art historians and all that, so it's a big part of what McKinley is. It has the McKinley Museum of Art, and across the street is the International Museum of Art! And students interact there all the time. I teach a course in American History and at one point in the course, we discuss when America became the center of the arts, in the 1950s, and talk about the art theorists of the time. The International Museum has one of the best collections in the country and in the world in American Expressionism. So I sent them over there. Here's this jewel across the street. They have to go see it. I have them read this fun little book Tom Wolf's *The Painted Word*, they shoot across the street and have to write papers and all of that. So try to use the assets of the area, like the museum, like the McKinley Museum on campus. So I think for lots of faculty members, the discipline connects with either the McKinley Museum or with the International Museum. Sending their students there or go there with their students and it's part of exposing them to these new worlds. We talked earlier before the taping began, when I was a kid discovering the Brooklyn Museum. A lot of people here recognize that a lot of our students have never walked into a museum so . . . I know a lot of my colleagues in the sciences will, kids will not only be doing their lab work but the sciences, and they'll send them over to the science museum here in town, or look at some works. I think a lot of the faculty, no matter what they teach whether it's Technology or Computer Information Systems or Literature or History or the Arts, have an awareness that many of our students, because of their social backgrounds, have not been exposed to this, haven't assimilated this into themselves, make sure that happens.

Tom is confident that McKinley faculty are ensuring that students are exposed to museums and the corresponding intellectual capital, but whether or not exposure is in fact encouraged by a large proportion of faculty, McKinley students, without an elaborated, intertexual discourse circulating throughout the campus itself, may never "assimilate this into themselves" and as a consequence, chances for social mobility upon leaving McKinley are greatly reduced.

The discourse surrounding art allows for the potential misinterpretation of McKinley as it is situated within the larger social field of higher education. As mentioned at the outset, the arts are indeed valued, but it is a matter of *how,* rather than a question of *if*—perhaps a subtle distinction, but a significant and powerful one nonetheless. In the absence of an elaborated discourse, valuation and appreciation circulate as a singular discourse as these messages become further embedded into the institution and into associated human bodies. In the excerpts provided here, though pulled from the context of interview transcripts, elaborated discourse is notably absent. At McKinley, the visual arts are discussed as a singular discourse in the absence of a developed vocabulary of the visual, and without intertextual referents. The arts, though "valued," exist in isolation from a larger universe of (highly valued) visual and literary texts. This singular discourse expressed by individuals and the institution (through text and collective voice) as part of its intellectual climate, separates and excludes McKinley students from the capital gains awarded through high levels of visual literacy.

LANGUAGE AND LITERACY AS ACADEMIC CAPITAL

Within the US system of higher education, visual literacy, communicated through legitimated academic language, is among the highly valued discourse of scholars—higher education's elite. Not unlike Brad, who in the introduction to this chapter struggled to find the word for sculpture, many McKinley students with whom I spoke embody a working-class habitus, shaped by the institution's working-class reputation, discourse of injured identities, and class-based bifurcation of knowledge. This embodiment not only positions students within the field of higher education, but it also aligns them with particular opportunity structures secured through the appropriation of particular kinds of academic capital. Language and literacies, as capital, or rather, as "discursive resources" (Hanks, 2005), and as products of individual and institutional habitus, structure students' trajectories. Brad's ambitions to "take pictures for National Geographic" upon graduation are indeed grand notions. This highly competitive position, like most, is not solely about the possession of a particular talent. It is about writing cover letters and other application materials, it is about credentials, field experience ("Freelancers usually come to us with at least five years of photojournalism experience or with specializations such as wildlife, underwater, nature, or aerial photography," http://www.nationalgeographic.com), and it is about interdisciplinary knowledge ("Our editors and photographers agree that it is important to complete a degree in a discipline other than photography" (http://www.nationalgeographic.com). At the time of our interview, months into his first semester at McKinley, Brad had yet to fill out his federal financial aid—forms and language that seem both unfamiliar and difficult for him to navigate, not unlike the visual arts.

As James Elkins (2008) asserts: "Visual literacy, or literacies . . . are as important for college-level education as (ordinary) literacy, and far less often discussed" (p. 1). In his argument for entitling his book *Visual Literacies,* Elkins reflects upon his reasons as to why this title was suitable. Following his first and second, his third rationale is based upon the lack of there really being anything better (or more appropriate). He states: "*Visual skills* is too narrow, because much of what matters here is politics, ideology, and history, as well as skills (p. 2)." Though without intention, Elkins gets at elite knowledge in his title—beyond skill, literacy is something of greater substance. Elkins's issue is that higher education remains text-based within our deeply visual culture. In other words, he is not advocating for the circulation of knowledge that is exclusionary. In fact, Elkins would prefer to see a visual learning model infused into all curricula and taught across all disciplines, and I would presume, within all universities; however, as skill and "greater substance" is continuously separated in practice within schools like McKinley, literacy of the visual kind that allows for the perception, evaluation, and articulation of objects and images (Elkins, 2008) would seem to run counter to the established model. For example, to "read" abstract or modern art is to see it as an object or image that does indeed hold value and meaning. But the legitimacy of abstract art has always had a class-based argument attached, reflecting the relationship between the working and lower classes and art as one that is based upon anti-intellectualism.

Again, I turn to Brad who communicates this distaste—emblematic of other students' articulation of abstract art:

AS: How important or valuable are the arts to your everyday life?
B: Very valuable and important. It really revolves around what I am going to do in the future so I really got to pay attention . . . can't just blow it off. Like I went to a local community college for criminal justice and I missed so many classes, and just dropped out, so here, I make sure I get up early, like no matter what. I have my girlfriend wake me up. I always get woken up by like 7:30, 8:00 and I usually get here by like 9 and my classes start between 10 and 11.
AS: So do you think you might check out the art galleries on campus?
B: I like looking at artwork, just not the crazy artwork like weird artwork. I don't get it. (mocking) "I can draw circles . . . or lines." I like real artwork, paintings and drawings and stuff.
AS: So more realistic types of things?
B: Yeah.
AS: Do you think the arts are important to every college student's experience?

B: It depends on their majors and their minors, like what they will do for their jobs, because why would you learn art if you need to know mechanics? There is no real sense to it, but if they want to, it won't hurt, but other than that, I don't really think it is too important.

For Brad, the arts are important to his future and to his everyday life—they are a means to a career in photography; again, Brad hopes to "take pictures for National Geographic." Brad talks about abstract art as 'crazy' and 'weird,' something that is not 'real' and does not hold any real meaning. This expression of distaste can be discussed as a kind of visual illiteracy, rather than a personal aesthetic preference. "As with reading comprehension, visually literate learners are able to make connections, determine importance, synthesize information, evaluate, and critique" (Frey and Fisher, 2008, p. 1).

The following interview material from a conversation with a professor of Economics and Director of the Foundations of Liberal Arts Program express-es perceptions of students' level of visual literacy at McKinley:

AS: Do you think that students at this institution value the arts? And if you could narrow that down to the visual arts, do you think that there's an appreci-ation?
I: No. Absolutely not. With the exception of those who know they already want to major in it, generally, it's not valued. If it's abstract they all think, "Oh, I could do that," and they don't see any depth in it. I don't think . . . I think their knowledge of it is very limited, so one of the things that we try to do in the course is try to point out, whenever possible, ways that visuals fit, that visual arts are arguments. They're non-discursive but they're still argu-ments. We're trying to get you to feel something, to view something different-ly, to . . . and maybe to create cognitive dissonance in a particular way. I mean, there are many, many different goals that artists have as many as there are artists. So it's . . . but they have no idea that that's there, they don't know what's there. They only see the . . . they only see the surface.

Arguably, visual literacy is part of the structure of habitus, but it also struc-tures habitus. The economics professor quoted above, a fourth generation PhD, is convinced students at McKinley do not value the arts (with the exception of fine arts majors). From his perspective, having grown up in a family with a deep appreciation for the arts as intellectual pursuit, he per-ceives students as having not only a different perspective of the visual arts, but one that is uninformed, limited in scope, and inexperienced. Below, this professor equates the ways in which students view the visual arts with the way they view books, something "mysterious" and "useless":

But I really, I think that students look at visual arts in a more extreme version the same way they look at my books. It's what the other does and it's mysteri-ous and needs to be cordoned off, you know . . . not valued but at the same time recognizing the elite value in it. So keeping those contradicting notions in mind and co-existing at the same is a difficult thing so you have to build these elaborate justifications around it. And I think that's what our students are, that's what they do. That's what they do with books and I think that's what they do with . . . to some degree with books, but I think that with the visual arts, it's far more extreme. It's far more . . . if you want a more pure case that would probably be it. Because the books, because they're in college, they have to read books, so it's kind of a little . . . not a pure taste, not as murky, more murky. Although advertising does create some muddy water in the other direction a little bit, but that they've got that organized in their minds. So art is useless stuff. It's not done for some other end; it's not instrumental in any way. That's how they look at it, so any knowledge that's not instrumental, I think, they have trouble with.

This conversation is emblematic of the mental and social structures imping- ing on students within this space. The individual habitus of students at McKinley, an institution with a working-class habitus, is presented here through the perception of a professor holding a position of professional and field-based authority—as the director of an academic program and tenured faculty member, but also as one who holds a highly valued degree of aca- demic capital (that which is desired within the intellectual field). This partic- ular professor distinguishes McKinley students as lacking in the academic capital that is valued within the academic field. This perceived deficiency (experiencing difficulty with "any knowledge that's not instrumental") fur- ther perpetuates the circulation of a discursive practice that may in fact be quite damaging to McKinley students, as well as students attending institu- tions with similar student demographics. Within this expression, students get caught up in a class-based web of discourse that influences the structure of curriculum, standards, expectations, and educational outcomes.

Not unlike the institutional messages discussed in previous chapters (of the rather distorted perception of the relationship between the working class and higher education), the institutional voice permeates every space of the campus, helping to form, establish, and legitimize the working-class reputa- tion and culture of the school as one that is limited. McKinley students and faculty, then, embody these messages. It is perceived, as the previous profes- sor of economics indicates, that these working-class students do not value the visual arts. This type of knowledge, like the knowledge disseminated by *his* books, is simply, "limited." As an institution, the College itself also commu- nicates valuation of the arts through what might be considered a singular discourse of appreciation. This excerpt from McKinley's website regarding the arts on campus articulates an emphasis upon the activities of artistic production, again, in the absence of intertextuality:

McKinley is known for its extensive programs in the visual, performing, and literary arts, providing many opportunities for students and members of the community to engage in a large variety of arts activities. These include plays and concerts, exhibitions and poetry readings, and include the areas of art conservation, art education, art history, ceramics, creative writing, dance, design, fiber design, furniture, interior design, jewelry, music, painting, papermaking, photography, printmaking, sculpture, and theater.

This may again seem all too subtle a distinction, but when positioned next to the institutional voice of a university at the highest end of the system hierarchy, subtleties begin to fade and reveal great contrast through these comparative measures:

> The arts abound at Harvard. Blending theory, practice, and passion across a diverse curricular and extracurricular landscape, Harvard is home to a vibrant and dedicated community which celebrates, interrogates, and practices art.
>
> The visual arts are found in abundance on Harvard's campus. The practice of the graphical, sculptural, digital, video, and mixed media arts thrive in the studios of Harvard's Department of Visual and Environmental Studies. A powerful tradition of art history, theory and criticism continues in the Department of the History of Art and Architecture. Student-led groups, visiting artists, gallery spaces, and a passionate community of artists all contribute to the dynamic culture of visual arts found on campus.

Harvard's articulation of the relevance of the arts on campus is structured around the practice of art and "a powerful tradition of art history, theory, and criticism." Harvard announces its legacy as "a vibrant and dedicated community which celebrates, interrogates, and practices art." The word choice and order suggest a serious commitment to the intellectual ends of art—its history, theory and criticism—always in conjunction with the practice of art. Harvard makes a point of blending theory and practice, as McKinley is "known for its extensive programs" in which students and members of its community engage in artistic activities—art history is listed among such "activities." The practice of art, the activity and physicality of its production, seem to exist in the absence of the kind of corresponding intellectual rigor and integration of various discourses/disciplines articulated by more elite institutions. With different institutional histories, habitus, and purposes, the visual arts remain an important component of each of these contexts of higher education, but as it is argued herein, the arts are valued in different ways—a consequence of the differentiation of knowledge, contributing to the preservation of inequality of opportunity. Again, the question of *how* the visual arts are valued becomes qualitatively relevant, particularly within a discussion of the production and dissemination of elite knowledge. Expressions of aesthetic valuation and experience become differentiated with the institutionalization and democratization of the visual arts. This institutionalization of the arts as elite knowledge is reproduced through two primary contexts: art museums and university art history programs, both established by a tradition of distinction.

DISTINCTIONS OF ART HISTORICAL DISCOURSE

The academic sphere of art is located within the relational fields of higher education and the art world. Art historians establish and legitimize particular types of art, as well as the ways in which they should be considered by their publics, to then disseminate within respective fields (granting degrees of symbolic capital to those able to appropriate this elite knowledge). Responsible for the production of scholarship as well as the production of popular texts, art historians can be "characterized by one or two extremes: they may write in either a mostly incomprehensible scholarly jargon or in a simplistic language that scrupulously avoids anything unexpected that might disturb the cultural canon" (Ebert-Schifferer, 2002, p. 46). In either case, art historical discourse remains, arguably, inaccessible to most. In its institutionalized form, art as academic capital need be examined across the fluid boundaries of these two fields. Though art history, as a discipline, has "undergone fundamental change" (Harris, 2001, p. 1) over the course of the past thirty plus years, becoming "much more open, interrogative (questioning), and self-critical than ever before" (Harris, p. 1), formal academic institutions "continue to use art history, like any other academic discipline, as a machine through which to 'process' students in order to 'produce' graduates claimed to be expert in certain skills, knowledge, and ways of thinking" (p. 2). These graduates have been trained, most often, to enter into the art world through careers as historians, curators, directors, and academics—reproducing the seemingly 'fixed' authority and truth of art-historical knowledge (Harris, 2001). This processing of students through formal art historical discourse continues to position the discipline among legitimized, elite knowledge. Harris (2001) highlights the "tensions between the critical intellectual openness of developments in art history and the continuing conservative institutional culture of academia over the past thirty years" (p. 2).

Though these tensions have demanded the consideration of art historians, institutionalized art history continues to re-establish and pursue the traditional aims of the discipline, prescribing to what Danto (1964) claimed long ago: "To see something as art requires something the eye cannot descry—an atmosphere of artistic theory, a knowledge of the history of art: an artworld" (p. 580). These intellectual properties, then, are located beneath the surface, a depth that the previously mentioned professor of economics discussed as something McKinley students are unable to pull forth. Becker (1982) also cites Danto's insight, using this to discuss the collaborative nature of the art world. Following Danto, Becker states: "Likewise, historians and scholars must establish the canon of authenticated works which can be attributed to an artist, so that the rest of us can base our judgments on the appropriate evidence" (p. 360). Though this authority has been challenged by scholars and those working within museums, art historical discourse continues to pervade as the highly valued knowledge of the elite.

Art historian Carol Duncan (1993) critiques this traditional, conservative approach to art history as establishment humanism, that which is arguably still taught within many elite liberal arts colleges, and those modeling the elite institutions.

> While extolling the value of individual creativity, it certifies creative activity only in the form of objects or acts produced for the contained spheres of the art world, implicitly justifying the absence of aesthetic values in so-called common experience. And while proclaiming the meanings of these objects and acts to be universal and theoretically available to all men, it turns its back on the fact that the physical and mental lives of most people are socially organized so that no matter how many free days the museums offer, they have neither the interest and training nor the social and geographical proximity with which to benefit from these supremely humanizing products. Thus establishment humanism protects and perpetuates the value of art in forms that insure its existence as a subculture, conserving both its authentic spiritual rewards and its real social prestige for the rich and those who serve them. (Duncan, 1993, p. 140)

Establishment humanism, which encourages aesthetic elitism, continues within institutions of higher education (as well as some private, elite high schools) as the traditional, pedagogical gold standard. This tradition originates within elite, private institutions of higher education, becoming a "discourse of distinction" (Gaztambide-Fernández, 2006). Duncan continues:

> Here, if anywhere, are the students whose backgrounds and future lives make relevant a classroom experience in which all art, past and present, is approached as if it were explicitly made to be looked at in the vacuum of the museum or acquired for one's own pleasure. Here, traditional, undergraduate art history finds its best audience as it presents the history of art as so many objects, bracketing and magnifying stylistic qualities, extolling the innate genius with which each great master solved a formal or iconographic problem, drawing an occasional parallel from philosophy or some other humanistic discipline, and extracting the World Views and Ideas that furnish the realm of abstract, universal truths—all the while avoiding or playing down the social matrix of art and turning the anti-art intentions of much twentieth-century art to aesthetic profit by treating them as 'formal advances' to be appreciated for their own sakes. (Duncan, 1993, p. 139)

Though perhaps the visual arts are not valued or discussed in the same *ways* at McKinley, or at similar institutions, as they are in more elite settings where the infusion of theory and practice is of greater emphasis (where elaborated cultural consumption circulates with elaborated discourse), the art history program at McKinley seems, not unlike the Honors Program, a bit of an anomaly in reference to the institution's working-class habitus. The program specifically defines itself as a discipline of the liberal arts (within the liberal arts college) and embeds itself within the 'discourse of distinction.' McKinley offers both a Bachelors degree in art history as well as an art history minor. As part of the Fine Arts Department, the art history program holds a small niche for students interested in studying the historical contexts of art in the Western world. With only a total of thirty-one students enrolled in its program during the 2008-2009 school year (twenty-eight are full-time), the program allows students to experience smaller class sizes and hold more personal relationships/mentorships with four faculty members that comprise the program. The excerpt below is taken from McKinley's website:

> The B.A. degree program in art history introduces students to the nature and history of artistic development in the Western world. This program is conceived as one of the disciplines of the liberal arts and is envisioned as a preparation for graduate study in art history, as well as for careers in art librarianship, museum work, slide curatorship, historic preservation, and art conservation. Art history majors are prepared to study art history, art conservation, and art administration in graduate school, or to begin careers as museum curators, consultants, and professionals in fields such as historic preservation, tourism, and cultural affairs. Graduates have been hired as curators, preparators, writers, and managers. Typical hiring firms include museums, galleries, auctioneers, publishers, art dealerships, public and cultural agencies, and universities.

Unlike other programs of study at McKinley, with the exception of Philosophy, receiving a graduate education is highlighted as part of students' training and future trajectory. Though other departments and programs that are part of the liberal arts mention graduate school or continuing education as an option for students pursuing their degrees, it does seem to be something of primary concern. For example, the English Department's B.A. program in Literature discusses post-undergraduate opportunities for their graduates—attending graduate school for literature is mentioned, last:

> Depending on their program and course concentrations, English graduates are prepared for business or public-sector positions requiring skills in writing, analysis, and problem solving. Graduates have been hired as proofreaders, assistant managers, Web designers, booksellers, and teachers. Typical hiring firms include publishers, retail businesses, and school districts. Recent graduates have been hired by companies such as Avalon Books, Barnes & Noble, White Directory Publishers, and Xcel Communications. Students who pursue advanced degrees in various disciplines may find themselves at a distinct advantage because of their well-honed communication skills. Students also may pursue advanced degrees in literature and become college professors.

Ava, a senior art history major, talks about the quality of her art history classes:

> AS: So how do the art history courses you have taken compare to your honors courses? Are there any glaring differences there?
>
> A: I would say that in general the questions that are asked . . . I mean . . .
>
> AS: What about expectations, standards?
>
> A: Well, standards in art history are more sky high than I think even my honors classes . . . well because they are looking for different things, they are really looking for different things in terms of . . . I think the more difficult professors, they are the true scholars and they have their expectations that I think are very traditional expectations. And they are nailing you on grammar, structure, everything. It is all written, and there is none of that bubble in the answer crap. So, whereas, I think some of the new art history professors are more lenient, they are looking more at your thought process. So maybe you don't have the best sentence structure in the world, but if you are getting your idea across, it won't kill you. Then you have the more traditional art history professors . . . Dr. Vaughn is my advisor, I actually always race her to class because we are always late, but I think they are a little more intimidating to students because they are just so intense and they are such unique people that I don't think a lot of the students know how to deal, whereas the newer art history teachers are a little more approachable. So in terms of expectations I think the older professors, more traditional, I think they have higher expectations.

Ava identifies the "true scholars" as those who have the highest standards—those who demand more than "bubble in the answer crap," describing them as "intense" and "a little more intimidating to students." Ava and Gail, friends who met through the art history program, were among the only students I interviewed to describe their professors as scholars, as intellectually intimidating, or held in high esteem. They were also among the only students to directly express an appreciation for high standards and for their experiences with intellectually challenging material and professors.

> A: Yeah, ummm, so I get frustrated, really frustrated, because I have learned so much more debating. I will actually remember the name of the painting and the date because we talked about it. So when the conversation dies and especially when you have a good professor leading it, that is what I don't get. I mean, if you have somebody droning on, he or she themselves don't truly expect someone to answer back. I get it, but that is what is so great about the art history professors, they are so passionate about their work. That is so cool. I mean, I am thinking, I am hanging around scholars . . . this is really awesome. I mean, how do I become one of you?

Art history professors, for Ava, model the kind of traditional academic model of impassioned scholarly behavior. Through this description, art history professors are also implicitly distinguished from other professors on campus as good, scholarly, and passionate. For Ava, art history, the program and its faculty, are held in great reverence—as a definitive image of "true," legitimate, superior scholarship. Art historical discourse at McKinley is reminiscent of an earlier, more elite model of higher education. This model, however, must be viewed in relation to the larger college community; both individuals also express disappointment in the caliber of student in their classes. Ava attributes this to the working-class culture of the city, and implicitly, to students' working class backgrounds, and to the working class reputation of the institution.

> A: This city is working class . . . is blue-collar for the most part. Unfortunately, that sometimes has an effect on a lot of students, that they are not as engaged in class. They think "it is just school, I will get it over with." It is not a time for them to really explore and discover something new about themselves. It is hard to critically think and to write, I am still battling with it, but I enjoy it. It is a good struggle because it has really helped me in other areas.

Within art history classrooms, as I observed, student responses and behaviors were similar to the responses and behaviors Gail and Ava described. Students in an upper-level elective course on twentieth-century art were rather unresponsive. Students appeared either uninterested or unprepared for class.

NOVEMBER, 2008

> Two female students in the front of the classroom are discussing applications for potential housekeeping jobs. The professor is not yet here.
> I noticed that one student has a laptop out to take notes and all other students have notebooks. There are several phones visible (out on desks). I look at the clock and the professor is 20 minutes late; however, the class does not seem to be too impatient. It is almost as though this is expected. After 22 minutes, the Professor strolls in and takes attendance. The student in front of me on the laptop is now checking Facebook.
> The professor continues, picking up from the previous class discussion with Cézanne and Van Gogh. She asks: What is the title of the piece? What is the date?
> All at once, a few tired voices in the front answer these data-driven questions.
> She (the professor) then asks: "What is the traditional meaning of still life?"
> An older student in front answers (inaudible from where I sit).

The professor replies: "Right, this is the meaning of it. So we should be aware of the duality—traditional still life calls attention to the passage of time (rotting fruit, etc.)."

A student sitting near me is now texting. The student on his laptop is still on Facebook.

The professor continues: "Cézanne is not interested in what is on the surface, but rather what is beneath the surface—the quest for the underlying meaning and truth, and he uses color and brushwork to do this." She continues: "Linear perspective (linear edge of table top) does not exist in Cézanne's work." "Who developed linear perspective and what did he do?"

There is no answer and she (professor) says: "This is art history II stuff." She is noticeably irritated. Moving on she states: "Realist work is a simple and reassuring version of reality (linear perspective is only an illusion, e.g. railroad tracks appear to be converging, but indeed, they are not)." She then asks: "What kind of lines . . . ?" Again, there is no answer.

Professor: "Does anyone know?" "This is art history II" (a prerequisite to this course). "This is terrible."

The professor then offers the answer. Students continue, distracted, occasionally looking up. The class continues in this way until students begin to pack up.

Both Gail and Ava, neither of whom were in this particular class, expressed frustrations with their peers and felt as though they needed to compensate for their classmates' lack of experience in classrooms such as this (those that try to engage students in the Socratic method).

Introductory art history classes allow for an interesting intersection of "elite knowledge" within a "non-elite" space as it is offered as a survey elective course—both majors and non-majors find their way to enormous lecture halls, together. With a majority of non-majors, art history 101 and 102 are elective courses offered to all McKinley students. I spoke with Amelia, an adjunct professor of art history about her introductory students:

Well I've gotten on the last, the first group of exams, I often get little notes on exams. And the last note I got was a clear indicator of that feeling it was somebody who wrote this huge letter about how they only take it because the college tells them they have to and they don't really care about art or art movement: "I'm an engineer." The first thing that they always say is, "Well I'm a Communications major, so I don't need this" or "I'm a whatever major" so there's no understanding from them that this fits into the broader spectrum of what education is suppose to provide. So I think almost on this level, for a lot of them, they almost treat their education like a vocational thing. They're here to get what they need to get through. They just don't understand why it's important.

In Amelia's classroom, the level of sincere interest was seemingly worse than that of the upper level art history class, as might be expected from a much larger elective class of non-majors who may not be as invested in this material:

OCTOBER, 2008

The instructor, a young woman finishing her Master's in Art History at State University, asks students to come forth to get their exams taken in the previous class.

One female student laughs and gestures to a friend to look at her score—I can't tell if it is high or low. The student next to me scored a 74 percent. The instructor announces that the class average was a 73 (10 points higher than last time). The students talk and compare grades and there is a lot of commotion. Finally, they are silenced by her asking them to stop talking (though she is fairly soft-spoken, particularly within this large lecture hall). The exam is multiple choice, something that this instructor was asked to implement after a previous semester of complaints that her exams were too difficult.

She (instructor) reads through specific questions that were noticeably problematic for students. She seems slightly irritated or perhaps frustrated? I am having difficulty hearing and wonder how students sitting in the back fair in a class this size. The questions asked consisted mostly of questions like: "What did you say the answer to number 35 was?"

The instructor soon offers extra credit after answering exam questions. The extra credit requires students to attend an event at a museum or gallery and write two pages about the exhibition or event—to give a personal response to an artwork or artist. She then says: "And they better be good . . . " She is then asked to repeat the assignment twice. In addition to the extra credit, she reminds students that she is also dropping the lowest test grade at the end of the semester. She then makes the announcement that in the last class someone had their head down on the desk—and said, "if you are going to do that, just leave. There is no need for that at this level."

My notes further indicate several students exiting the class at different times during lecture to leave early. "They (students) slip out through doors at the sides of the lecture hall when the instructor turns her back to write particular terms on the board." "Some walk straight out, past the instructor, and through the front of the lecture hall nearly thirty minutes into the class." The instructor was reasonably frustrated with students' behavior and had to stop several times to ask that students stop talking. From my tucked away perspective, students were not just uninterested or unprepared, but they were not taking any notes. In fact, many did not even pretend to take notes as I witnessed other students doing—they visibly slept. I found this to be somewhat alarming, but was not terribly surprised, given the rather low average on their most recent multiple-choice exam.

THE RELATIVE CONCEPT OF "ELITE": ART HISTORY IN CONTEXT

Art history as a discipline does not seem to fit within the same "working-class" reputational framework expressed by professors and students from the cross-section of McKinley's campus. Art history requires students to learn and practice a discourse that holds particular distinction as a form of elite knowledge within the field of cultural production, of which higher education is a part. Though this distinction is somewhat evident at McKinley, within the larger field of higher education, it does not hold the same distinction of art history departments and programs at more prestigious colleges and universities. Differentiation exists here in more covert ways, and is again, more visible through a comparative lens, where the concept of art history as elite knowledge appears relative to context and discourse.

The pedagogical methods familiar to and often associated with and practiced within elite liberal arts colleges tend to be Socratic (Gaztambide-Fernández, 2009; Semel, 1992). Gaztambide-Fernández (2009) asserts:

> Elite boarding schools are characterized by a Socratic approach to pedagogy that is rare in other schools. This is so not because other educators do not value this approach to teaching, but because teaching at elite boarding schools is premised on two implicit assumptions: first, that the great majority of classes are small, and, second, that the students who come into the classroom have been preselected through the admissions process. . . . Unlike the vast majority of public schools, these students (and teachers) have been carefully preselected through an elaborate process of exclusion to ensure that they are not only able but eager to engage in the seminar style of teaching that has become "the central classroom metaphor of the boarding school." (Gaztambide-Fernández, 2009, p. 30)

Although questions were used to generate discussion or establish meaning at McKinley, they often fell flat on an unassuming audience. The classroom itself was unable to maintain discussion and seemingly unable to answer simple (fact-based) questions posed by the professor. The environment was unable to sustain the level of conversation requested, and it is within the classroom where we see the greatest differences. Within these classrooms, though the professor engaged in a kind of Socratic pedagogical approach, learning did not espouse ways of thinking, but reinforced *what to think*. Returning to the elite secondary boarding school classrooms, which mimic those of smaller, elite private colleges, Khan (2008) describes certain levels of discussion that encourage and teach one to "think through the world," as opposed to "teaching students about the world" (p. 203). As mentioned in the previous chapter, teaching students "how" to think, instead of "what" to think, "endow(s) students with marks of the elite" (Khan, 2008, p. 206). In the above classroom observation note, I am again alerted to subtleties of differentiation. Questions posed by a female professor of art history, who was named by art history majors as among the most esteemed, were of a one-dimensional, fact-based nature. These kinds of questions do not teach students *how* to think, but *what* to think.

To get at the qualitative intricacies of differentiation among McKinley's art history program and that of more elite institutions, I turn once again to a comparative perspective derived from core class documents (syllabi, specifically course requirements). A comparative perspective of these documents not only allows for explicit differences to surface, but also illuminates hidden and implicit forms of the unequal distribution of elite knowledge. As an example of curricular differentiation, syllabi tell us a great deal about the ways in which particular courses are structured. I begin by comparing introductory level survey courses. Because these courses are open electives and tend to be rather large, they implicitly suggest the college's expectations of and standards for *all* students. Each semester, McKinley offers two sections of Introductory Art History. The first section, Art History 101, covers, in chronological order, the Stone Age to the Middle Ages, and the subsequent section addresses the art of the Renaissance through the Modern Era. The particular art history 101 syllabus under consideration is one that was created by the same aforementioned professor held in high esteem by art history majors. The syllabus identifies the required textbook: *Gardner's Art Through the Ages: A Western Perspective.* In contrast, the syllabus at a private, higher-ranking institution, lists the required text as *Art History* by Stokstad; however, this introductory art history course also requires "additional online readings" and offers an extensive list of suggested readings, which includes essays, articles, and books by such authors as Geertz, Baxandall, Vasari, Panofsky, Duncan, Krauss, and Berger. Berger's *Ways of Seeing* (1990), now considered a classic text, continues to influence interdisciplinary thinking and is often used in undergraduate education as a basic primer on visual literacy. Considered an approach to the 'new language of images' (Murray, 2003, p. 45), Berger's "principal aim . . . was 'to start a process of questioning'" (Murray, 2003, p. 45). Having met its principal aim, this small, "accessible" text continues to initiate new ways of seeing for readers in all disciplines.

Perhaps most strikingly, the syllabus from the higher ranking institution begins with the depiction of two images—Divinci's *Mona Lisa* juxtaposed with Warhol's *Mona Lisa* (1963).

As this imagery introduces the course syllabus, one might expect material to be taught using a visual, analytic approach and a vocabulary requiring higher degrees of visual literacy. Students are asked, at the outset, to engage in visual communication, to analyze, and to draw from multiple lines of discourse (art history, theory, cultural studies, etc.). The course description, which immediately follows these images, reinforces the relevance of this visual juxtaposition:

> This course is an introduction to western art history focusing mainly on European art produced between the Renaissance and the present day. It will provide an overview of canonical works of art as well as an understanding of some issues in the construction of art history and appreciation for different points of view. The course will develop skills in analysis of works of art and the ability to see how works connect with the time in which they were created.

In comparison, McKinley's syllabus lists seven objectives for students. This list of objectives indicates a linear approach to pedagogy and the dissemination of knowledge, evoking the differentiation of knowledge and pedagogy espoused by Anyon's (1981) study on *social class and school knowledge*. In addition, the McKinley course ends with modern art, while the comparative class moves into the postmodern and into the contemporary. The comparative class also emphasizes multiple approaches to art history, while critiquing art history itself, and introduces multiple points of view—expanding thought, language, discourse, and intertextual learning. In addition, the comparative syllabus lists more demanding requirements: readings, online responses, two short papers, a mid-term and a final exam. The McKinley course, on the other hand, requires attendance and the successful completion of three multiple-choice/true/false exams (lowest grade dropped). Perhaps more importantly, the McKinley course omits the construction of Art History as discipline. Without the knowledge of the construction of the field itself, as well as an emphasis on different points of view, students miss "insight into the system" that structures their social realities (Anyon, 1981, p. 37). This insight is the kind of powerful, critical knowledge that often leads to transformative practice.

Other components of the McKinley syllabus evoke Anyon's (1981) classroom distinctions and demonstrate higher education's version of working-class classrooms as related to discipline. "Please note that this body of material and these objectives are considered basic to any college education all over the world." Another statement reminds students they are in a college classroom: "You are required to understand from the very beginning that this is a college classroom, and you are expected to be here solely for the purpose of learning art history." These statements enforce "proper behavior in class." It is clear that this professor believes McKinley students need consistent reminders such as this to behave properly in a college classroom.

Within McKinley, honors students are distinguished from non-honors, and art history majors seem to be of a different caliber of student. Absorbed within the elite knowledge of art history, these students use a more academic language in conversation, they are trained more specifically to pursue graduate education, and express a more sophisticated visual literacy. Outside of their majors, participant honors students exist among students they assume are there just to get a degree and speak with little regard for their classroom behavior and intellectual contributions. In this environment, art history students, just as all other students at McKinley, come up against class-based structural inequality. In an environment that does not truly mimic the learning environment of more elite programs, students cannot truly receive a qualitatively equal education or benefit from the same opportunities.

Within the context of McKinley, art history students' educational experiences seem to be infused with tensions and contradictions—perhaps it is a matter of the "appropriation of space"? Outside of their smaller intellectual communities, they sit in classes with other students who do not appear interested, disrespect instructors and professors, and do not bring the same kinds of educational training to the classroom, which allows for rigorous, engaging classroom learning experiences. As a result, though aspirations may be similar, future trajectories appear to be slightly different. Gail hopes to attend graduate school, but had not applied anywhere by the Fall of her senior year, and she had not taken the GREs. She hopes to specialize in French Romanticism, but has not studied the French language.

G: I am totally going to grad school. I am looking at Case Western, Temple and OSU, which I know is kinda like an undergrad kind of school, but I really like their program. They have a really good art history graduate program. I mean I know that when I was in high school, that was like, the party school.
AS: Yeah, I am sure grad school is a different scene—and now you are going for art history?
G: Yes, and um, I would like to specialize in French Romanticism. I have always had a thing for that, so my project over the summer is to really, really learn French.
AS: Wow . . .
G: Yeah, so I am getting the Rosetta Stone, but it is so hard because I grew up with my family speaking Italian, because my grandmother hardly spoke English. So learning French is completely different. But here I am, wanting to specialize in French Romanticism and I can't speak French.
AS: So you don't speak any French?
G: Well, no, but in my classes you need to know some French terms and you know, I can recognize some things, but no, I am definitely in the beginning stages.
AS: And have you applied anywhere yet for graduate school?

G: No, I mean I still have a year and I still have to take the GRE's, but I am going to wait until next semester to get really official. I have done some preliminary stuff, like looking things over.

Language requirements for art history majors in other institutions, such as those for incoming first-year graduate students at Harvard, are:

> For all fields, the Department's minimum language requirement is a reading knowledge of two languages that are relevant to the student's field of study and research interest (excluding his/her native language). The languages will have to be deemed necessary, and approved of, by a faculty member in the field and the DGS. The student will be required to provide proof of proficiency in the languages (www.gsas.harvard.edu).

At McKinley, the Art History Program (and also the Honors Program in both cases) does not provide an adequate level of undergraduate education to enable students to move into elite graduate schools. Though these students seemed confident, bright, ambitious, and optimistic about their futures, they are positioned as both dominant and dominated within the field of higher education, which is positioned within the field of power to function as both inclusive and exclusive. Ava also plans to go to graduate school, but is following her true passion and pursuing a career in theater. This is Ava's last year and she has auditioned for several graduate programs within the United States, but was not accepted to any of the schools to which she applied. Ava will attend a program in Scotland instead that she said, "just fell into her lap." And though she seemed thrilled to have the opportunity to travel and study theater overseas, the prospect of attending the American schools on her list quickly diminished.

In addition to the art history department, the McKinley Museum of Art stands as the only other campus-centered context for the overt dissemination of the visual arts. In an effort to understand the potential motives for the building of and investment in the $33 million McKinley Museum of Art, it is worth assessing public communication relating to the reasons the College might have been interested in investing in an art museum. However, it is also important to note that institutions often self-promote to bolster their ranking and image, choosing to publish or highlight particular information, while leaving out context or conflicting information that may contradict stated claims. With this in mind, speculation is required to consider the following rationale.

We know institutions in higher education, as well as those within the arts, have been forced to compete within their respective, homologous fields. Part of competing means improving offerings and bolstering resources for potential students. Like so many other American colleges and universities, McKinley has been characterized by recent growth. The McKinley News reported that over the last 10 years, the student academic profile has improved while enrollment and the number of faculty hires has increased. In addition, the McKinley News reported that the campus experienced numerous capital improvements, which includes a $350 million expansion project to begin the summer of 2010. But why invest in a $33 million art museum? Even though a significant portion of this money was acquired through a private donation, the building of this structure required significant fundraising and physical and mental labor on the part of McKinley staff. McKinley's President offers an answer to this question prior to the building of the new structure:

> We've always been very strong in the arts. We're now looking at the construction of a new McKinley Museum of Art facility. This will enhance the museum's exhibition spaces and will expand its ability to interact with our academic programs.

At the Museum's opening ceremony, the President (also a museum Board member) stated:

> This enables us to continue our oldest tradition of excellence in the arts. The museum is a superb validation of the power of a partnership that is both public and private. We will be a premier destination for artists, educators, and students alike.

It would seem as though the McKinley Museum of Art is an extension of a "tradition of excellence in the arts," but what other motivating factors may have contributed to the decision to invest the college's resources into the building of a new art museum, particularly as the new museum is a new *location* for a museum that already existed? Was the positioning of the McKinley Museum, a culture-dispensing institution, fodder for the repositioning of McKinley College? The museum, however, as a public space for the appreciation of the visual arts, occupies a rather precarious position on a "working-class" campus. It is to this position I now turn.

THE MCKINLEY MUSEUM OF ART

> Anyone observing the Sunday crowds at the National Gallery of Art in Washingon, DC, or at the Metropolitan Museum of Art in New York might assume, from the casual attire and informal manner of the gallery goers, that visitors to American art museums represent a cross-section of American society. I would argue that the reverse is true: that the museum in the United States, far from welcoming all visitors, attracts some and repels others, and

that it does so on the basis of class; I would also argue that the class biases of these major cultural institutions are inscribed within and reinforced by the space of the museum itself. (Wallach, 2002, p.114)

Just as art museums are bound to their history of elitism through the dissemination of elite knowledge, they are also bound to the more contemporary and contradictory ideas of democratization and accessibility—an unavoidable tension in the present day social and economic position of cultural institutions. Art museums must walk a delicate line between being accessible and appealing to a more general audience, while also appealing to those who easily navigate art in its institutionalized form. As a result, "Art museums have experienced a "crisis of identity" as their "essential underlying function, according to sociologists like Bourdieu, is to validate unequal social and economic statuses in society" (Plattner, 1996, p. 60). In *The Field of Cultural Production* (1993), Bourdieu suggests that art institutions cultivate, perpetuate, and conceal a certain readability of art objects in order to include individuals "who have the means to appropriate it" while excluding those who do not. Bourdieu concludes: "only a few have the real possibility of benefiting from the theoretical possibility, generously offered to all, of taking advantage of the works exhibited in museums" (p. 234). Art museums have been challenged on this assertion since the sixties, employing, not unlike higher education, democratizing efforts to increase access. It would seem as though these efforts have accomplished this more recent mission: "attendance at American art museums rose from twenty-two million in 1962 to over one hundred million in 2000; more than half of our art museums were founded after 1970 and new museums are opening and existing museums are getting bigger and bigger" (Cuno, 2004, p. 17). In fact, despite the recent economic recession, 2009 statistics collected by the American Association of Museums report increases in attendance among the majority of American museums, of all types, budgets, and within all regions (with the exception of New England) (Katz, 2010). If rising attendance numbers alone indicate the success of democratization, then it would appear as though art museums, like higher education, have reached their institutional goals. However, and again, not unlike efforts to democratize higher education, increasing numbers of museum visitors arguably hide the fundamentally unequal, and relatively stable structure of these homologous fields.

THE MCKINLEY MUSEUM OF ART: DISRUPTIVE PRESENCE AND OVERWHELMING ABSENCE

Like other art museums, the McKinley Museum of Art appears to make sincere efforts to respond to socially-driven pressures to increase its level of accessibility for its students, faculty, and to the larger community. McKinley offers educational programming, docent-led tours, among other programs designed to engage the broader community, and in 2008, the Museum hired an individual specifically for these purposes ("Curator of Public Engagement"). Robin, a curator at the McKinley Museum of Art, discusses the relationship between McKinley College and the Museum:

> That's another interesting question. I'm sure that in relation to some of the other colleges you might be speaking to for this study, the Museum is kind of a hybrid, kind of an anomaly. Most times the museum that is situated on a college campus is part of the college program. Entirely financed by, whatever they are, private/public. We're in between. We have our own 501C3 designation, so we're incorporated independently, so we have a board of trustees who have fiduciary responsibility; yet, the building is a campus building that is given to us rent-free, our maintenance crew is state funded, the director and a few of the positions, not many, are state positions, with state salaries and state benefits, and I am on the other side. More of us are not state people, and that was strategically done in the past so that we could become eligible as one of a few institutions that is, for example, eligible to submit grants to the American State Council in the Arts. Because the state support versus every other kind of support is balanced in the kind of way that if the state is low enough that they don't feel like it is one state institution giving to another and there's a conflict of interest. So we are this kind of strange hybrid that is part campus, part community and it's this kind of balance back and forth. The state has invested quite a few of the millions of dollars that it's taking to do this building. I think out of thirty-five, they're at least eight and probably going to be more than that, so you know the more and more you're going to be hearing the combined title "The Museum of Art at McKinley College." We already do that, but I think there is going to be more of an effort to creating the identity that it is very linked to the college. At the same time, we're always gesturing to the outer community that we are here to serve all of New York and we need your support to do that, too. So it is this kind of curious mix.

The McKinley Museum of Art (MMA), as part of the McKinley campus, has struggled somewhat in the past to establish a meaningful relationship with students and faculty (as discussed in faculty and staff interviews), and this struggle seems to ensue. At the time of most of the student interviews, the MMA was transitioning into its new space (refer to chapter 3 for a descrip-

tive analysis). The presence of the building was, and is undeniably "there," as
the architecture occupies an enormous, sweeping space at the entrance to the
campus, but discussions with students indicate its overwhelming absence.

Perhaps the most alarming data regarding the relationship between students and the MMA is found among the level of unawareness of the building
itself. This is supported by the number of students, both in and outside of the
arts, who have never seen the inside of the MMA, and those who are unfamiliar with its existence (even after the immense new architectural structure
of the MMA was erected at the entrance to the campus as discussed in
chapter 3). Ben, an undergraduate student majoring in Sociology says this:

> AS: What do you think about the new art building?
> B: I never went to the New Museum.
> AS: Is there much talk about that on campus?
> B: Not at all.
> AS: Not at all? Do people know what it is, do you think?
> B: I don't think so. There was one of my friends that was excited for it and
> she's an art major but that's pretty much it.
> AS: Do you think that McKinley places emphasis on the arts as a valuable
> component of your education?
> B: I don't honestly see it. I know it's known to be a fairly decent arts school
> but I think that's only a very small basket. There are pieces of art all over the
> place but those don't have any kind of importance to us.

Erica mimics Ben's response:

> AS: Now I don't know if you've seen that big building?
> The one you thought was going to be a parking ramp?
> That is now the McKinley Museum of Art.
> E: Is it open yet?
> AS: No. It's not opening for a while.
> E: Is it still in the other building for now?
> AS: No it's closed.
> E: No, definitely not. I haven't been there since I was a kid. I remember I
> always had good experiences. Wasn't it kind of a history part to it though? I
> remember, something, or was I just losing it? I don't know. It's been a while.
> It's sad, that these things are on campus and you just don't always know.
> AS: What do you think the perception is on campus of the MMA and of the
> arts? In general . . . I know you're not in an arts department, but what's the
> general perception of students and faculty on campus?
> E: To be honest, nobody has ever really talked about it. Yeah. I think maybe
> one teacher mentioned it once, but it wasn't a huge conversation. Um, I mean
> there's probably no reason for education or math teachers to mention it, but
> like, even when people talk about it, or talk about art in general, they don't
> really mention the one on McKinley campus. I didn't realize what it was
> called. I haven't been there in years, that's why I never really thought about it.

AS: So you're not hearing too much from people on campus about the new building either?

E: No, no. I haven't really heard anything about it. I didn't even know it was going to be an art museum until I saw the sign. Yeah, so I think that maybe they should advertise a little more because there's . . . I haven't seen any signs or anything. So, but no, I haven't. Nobody talks about, like art on campus. Maybe that's just my classes or you know, cause I know people I go to school with are art majors and they do art, art is their concentration for education or something like that, and they love to talk about art, but no one ever mentions the one on McKinley, which is kinda weird.

AS: Does it feel like it's part of the College?

E: Maybe non-existent cause like I said, no one ever talks about it, so, it does feel like it's not a part of the college cause you don't hear about it or like "have you checked this out on campus yet?" It feels like it's kinda just out there. It's one of those things on campus that no one really thinks to go to.

AS: Right. And it's right on the perimeter of the school.

Christine demonstrates a similarly limited knowledge of the Museum on McKinley's campus:

AS: Talk about the expansion.

C: I have no idea what's going on. They don't talk about it. All I know is that it's going to be an art building.

AS: So they are not really promoting it?

C: No, not at all. Which is kind of sad, cause it looks really nice.

AS: And you're in the arts?

C: Not yet. I haven't taken any art classes yet at McKinley. Only the fashion arts. Well, I have friends in them and they are just kind of a little bit talking about it. They're like "oh, it's the new art building." My friend that goes to State University knows more about it than I did.

Interestingly, the President of McKinley has a different perspective of student awareness:

AS: Do you feel that students, in general, value the arts at McKinley?

President: I think so. They are very aware of the New Museum of Art, they'll have events there, and they have to because they have all these students in their classes. Whether it's the visual or the performing arts, and if you go into the residence halls (and we've been upgrading them) and the students have drawn all over the walls—beautiful, professional drawings. Or if you go into the Science [building], which we're going to be renovating, there are amoebas and everything else all painted all over the walls. I mean, that's all student art and student creativity . . . If you work on a group project in the class, the artistic kids really help you in developing your project and your initiatives. So I can tell if I'm teaching a class and there's an artistic kid in a group of others. They really bring their experiences and it makes a much more interesting project quite often. So, I think that they are aware, they know they're getting a new art museum.

Visitor statistics for 2009 indicate that only 7.6 percent of visitors are from the city of Arkive, again a city that suffers from its economic and racially segregated position. Zip code data show that the largest percentage of visitors come from outside of the immediate county in which Arkive is located. Conversations with the person responsible for keeping statistics at the Museum indicate that most of the admissions are "regular admissions," followed by seniors, members, and then McKinley students (who receive free admission to the Museum). That McKinley students capture the smallest percentage of visitors to the Museum is yet another indication of its absence in campus consciousness. Though the Museum has made great efforts to increase awareness and attendance, particularly among McKinley students, numbers indicate that these efforts fall short.

Sheila, Curator of Public Engagement, reflects upon her perceptions of the MMA through her previous employment at the International Museum (located directly across the street from the MMA) and the failed relationship with McKinley College:

> S: In the past year, cause I'm new, I'm at one year. And really being across the street from The International Museum, I never crossed over. I never came over here, and I worked there for over 10 years. I never crossed the street more than once or twice.
> AS: Why is that?
> S: I don't know. Once I got over here, I realized they have a cool community. The International Museum is missing out! Now The McKinley Museum of Art is it! Cause it is! When you come here, and you have to come early cause of parking, you really do have this cool community that comes, and has a little bit of time to like walk around, or the staff to see each other, because you have already put in extra hours (laughing). But The Museum of New Art and McKinley College, in my opinion, of being here not very long, is that there is never been a collaboration that has been welcoming holistically. What I mean by that is that there are a few staff members that collaborate all the time with McKinley but it's the same faculty over and over and over. They have built up a friendship, they play music together, they watch films together, but that's not what I want. I want that group to continue, but 12 other groups to happen, 20 other groups to happen. No one has ever reached out to all of McKinley. No one has reached out and said, "this is for you, too" and I'm not sure why.

Again, Robin reiterates Sheila's perception of this failed relationship:

> AS: Can you talk about the relationship between the museum and the rest of college? What is it like?
> R: How the institution has been perceived by the college faculty and students? I've actually been a little surprised at what a hard sell it has sometimes been to get students over here. People in fine arts, they don't walk across the street to the International Museum either. It has sometimes been a bit of struggle to get on the orientation tours. People might do their tours outside our front doors

and say "and this is the art museum" and move on without coming in. We would try to have these cultivation lunches or breakfasts and invite people from orientation and say "come in, come and see what we're all about, bring your group." It'll take 5 minutes to walk through some of the spaces so people know we're here. And some people are good at it, and some people aren't. Again, I think there's a lot of optimism that since we're kind of up on the third floor, we're kind of hard to find, people have a hard time with the parking and all of that. The new building is going to just make life a lot easier and people are going to be curious about what's inside our building and want to come in. So things have changed over the years. I think the staff is getting savvier in ways we might be able to intersect. We have some new staff that of course bring fresh ideas, Sheila is very good about different approaches to learning, not your traditional art education in the museum. There are some things, some steps we've taken along the way. So I think these are all things that show the museum is growing and maybe in its early years it seems sort of like the "Arkive club." To say that, I don't want to conjure up that kind of private club in terms of Arkive elite, but the International Museum might be inaccessible to some people and I think MMA has always seemed like a place where everyone is welcome. A lot of people describe the museum that way. That people are friendly, and they feel like they can belong here, but maybe in the early years things were a bit more conservative. We're trying to reach every kind of interest and audience and really try to reach out into the community, so I think as the concept of the museum has grown and the creativity of the people involved with it, including the people from the college interacting with programs, and we'll be doing more academically in terms of lectures and different kinds of presentations.

Though staff at the MMA follow patterns that express the sincere, altruistic desire to democratize the institutionalization of the visual arts (at least in terms of their immediate context), their efforts seem to coarsely rub up against the boundaries of a different cultural field and perhaps a different institutional habitus. The McKinley Museum is perceived by many of the students with whom I engaged as a disruptive presence (for example, one student said the Museum space "should've been a parking garage"), but the Museum also maintains an overwhelming absence in the space of campus consciousness. There is certainly nothing wrong with the desire for better facilities (e.g. more parking spaces), particularly at McKinley, where there is a rather large percentage of commuter students, and there is nothing necessarily wrong with a general disinterest in art museums, but as Bourdieu so brilliantly determines, a love of art is part of habitus. The symbolic boundaries built up around the McKinley Museum of Art and McKinley College are created by a forcefield of capital and value-laden knowledge—capital that is not shared within these separate domains. If distance seems great between these institutions that occupy the same immediate geography, it is because a rather large symbolic rift exists between these institutions that are at once part of the same field of power but also of their own distinct fields.

A central argument made by Bourdieu, among others, regards entry and visitor comfort in the space of the museum:

> They [visitors] are aware on some level that the museum represents an authority that stands over and above them. Consequently, their comfort or discomfort will depend rather directly upon the extent to which they identify with that very official, if anonymous, authority. Such identification, however, is not a matter of identifying with bourgeois power per se . . . the authority that presides over the museum presents itself in the guise of a benevolent promoter of the arts. Visitors are thus exhorted to identify not with the museum authority itself, which would be difficult given its tendency towards anonymity, but with its claims to society's highest values—values associated with art, culture, and civilization. (Wallach, 2002, p. 124)

But there must first be entry—something in which most McKinley students (based upon Museum statistics) are not participating. Before entering the McKinley Museum, though it would be wrong to assume any level of consciousness involved in the decision, potential visitors must first confront the ideology of the museum (e.g. the class-based discourse inscribed in its architecture). This fraught territory (approaching the museum), for McKinley students, seems to be one that is contradictory to their lives, and as such, becomes part of the structure of inequality.

Arguably, art museums, even with their increasing attendance numbers, hold on to privileged class biases, which are "inscribed within and reinforced by the space of the museum" (Wallach, p. 114). On a campus that serves a largely working-class student body, these biases (which are also arguably evident in the architecture and symbolic existence of museums, caught in a historical web) seem to inhibit the crossing of culture and contribute to the reproduction of structure of social class and its related hierarchy of knowledge. Despite more recent efforts to break with an elitist tradition, art museums "remain engines of inclusion and exclusion" (Wallach, p. 122).

CONCLUDING THOUGHTS

In conclusion, I return to Brad, the fine arts major whose words introduced the material and set the trajectory for this chapter. Brad, like other working-class McKinley students and the institution itself, expresses class through a language and disposition that is indicative of the proliferation of a singular discourse. This discourse, as part of both individual and institutional habitus, is not to be understood as bereft of culture, knowledge, or meaning, but one that is different from that which 'bears on the social definition of the (elite) speaker.' However much Brad values the visual arts, his level of visual literacy does not allow him to traverse the space of various types of knowledge; however, McKinley, as a "working-class" institution, is unable (because of its own position in the larger field) to offer its students elite knowledge with all of its privilege attached. Duncan (1993) concludes:

> Teachers in public colleges may protest that many of their students demonstrate high interest and capacity in art appreciation in spite of nonsupportive family backgrounds. I am sure they do. But what happens to them after they leave college and enter their working lives? Unless they join up with the intellectual establishment and thus escape the work world—and this requires exceptional skills and mobility—most of them will have neither the opportunities nor the interest to involve themselves with art on a continuing basis. It does not necessarily follow that they are any the poorer for being deprived of high culture *as our institutions define it*. (Conversely, I am not arguing that "low" or mass culture is therefore good art.) My point here is that institutions that claim to disseminate high culture to the masses do not fulfill their claims (p. 142).

NOTE

1. Studio art, located within fine art departments or as part of visual art departments, is separated here for the purpose of my argument. Both studio art and art history demand levels of visual literacy, but this is where an important distinction begins. Studio art emphasizes the production of art objects/images and art history emphasizes the critique and evaluation of those objects and images.

Chapter Six

Re-Conceiving Democratization

> But if "democratization" is taken to mean what it always implicitly suggests, namely the process of equalization of educational opportunities for children from the different social categories (perfect equality of opportunity presupposing that all subcategories should have a rate of opportunity equal to the overall rate of enrollment for that age group), then the empirically ascertained increase in the chances of all categories does not in itself constitute a sign of "democratization." (Bourdieu, 2000, p. 224)

The pages of this book are cast in class because class, it seems, is everywhere. It spans the length of billboards and broadcasts itself in the media, up close, right in the face of things. It runs through the city and down its segregating highways. It manifests unabashedly on Wall Street and heaps on the corner of Main Street. It has a color. It is what you eat; it is how you eat. It resounds through language and its jurisdiction is knowledge. It shapes reputation. It opens and closes doors. It is a roving eye, never dormant. It is with us until the end—in sickness and in health—lengthening or shortening that span. And though seemingly omnipresent, it remains strangely absent from the collective conscious.

Class, as a lived concept, is nebulous and difficult to define, and in part, this helps to explain its absence. As class has moved from the periphery to the center of scholarly discussions, many continue to struggle over "the way it works" (Weis, 2008), "how it works" (Aronowitz, 2004; Lareau & Conley, 2008), and how it is "divided" (Brantlinger, 2003). But, as Michael Zweig (2000) asserts: "the lines—what is rich, what poor, what middle—is largely arbitrary" (p. 3). However arbitrary, nebulous, and seemingly fluid class may be, it is deeply felt and deeply embedded in the structure of social space. In a word, it "matters" (hooks, 2000; Keller, 2005). Scholarship tells us that class is worth the intellectual struggle, particularly in times uncertain—times that indicate a structural metamorphosis that further aggravate the unequal patterns of the past. Weis (2008) suggests: "Such recognition of both the structuring effects of class and the ways in which class is lived out has never been more pressing, given key shifts in the global economy and accompanying deepening social inequalities" (p. 3). As competition for academic capital continues to grow and the importance of postsecondary degrees (with increasing attention paid to where those degrees are from) becomes increasingly important to both institutional and individual class positioning, income inequality and educational achievement gaps between the rich and poor follow suit, even as racial gaps narrow (Reardon, 2011). Set against a backdrop of greater access, growth in income-based gaps in college entry, persistence, and graduation (Baily & Dynarski, 2011) underline a deep contradiction—one that is difficult to ignore. And yet, even with all critical fingers pointing towards social class as a clear marker of inequality, it remains largely removed from the discourse of everyday life. So when does *Homeless* really make its way *to Harvard*? Put another way, when does class really make its way from billboard to collective conscious?

Answering these questions requires vision that extends far beyond the campus of McKinley College, and far beyond that of Harvard University. As a case study, it would be erroneous to view McKinley in an isolated context, cut off from its situated position within social space. As part of the expansion and democratization of higher education, McKinley and those associated with the institution are part of the structure and structuring of unequal, hierarchical social space. As such, the research and implications produced within McKinley College resonate loudly beyond its immediate location. At the center of this research, democratization cuts away from McKinley and across an expanse that includes multiple institutions and fields. As discussed herein, both institutions of higher education and the institutionalized sector of the art world (e.g., art museums) have responded to the public's call to democratize and each has been charged with similar outcomes that reproduce, rather than reduce, class-based inequality. And though democratization is, as Duncan (1993) describes, a "laudable goal," it is also "one that rests on rather a shaky assumption: that it is possible to democratize an elitist, liberal arts education" (Duncan, p.135). In the interest of uncovering the mechanisms through which the social process of democratization, as currently conceived, preserves and perpetuates inequality within the system of higher education, this book explored the vestiges of this process through McKinley College.

ENDURING REPUTATIONAL *AFFECTS*

Reputational *affect* allows for a better understanding of the involvement of habitus. Student participants' perception of one another, and potentially of themselves, as well as participating faculty perceptions of students, communicate the larger Discourse of the institution and that of the system of higher education, one that marks McKinley students as intellectually inferior to students positioned within colleges and universities of higher rank and reputation. Transformation requires a newly imagined reality of McKinley and a steady reversal of its current reputation. As Professors become "socialized" into a faculty culture that seems to mark McKinley students as lacking, and as a result, lowers standards and expectations, students have the potential to internalize these messages, which also happen to parallel larger messages about the school itself and their (expected) place within higher education. These discursive patterns have the power to naturalize reputation as a marker of identity, and in this case, as one that remains perceived as injured, incapable, and intellectually inferior. These imagined social facts of and surrounding McKinley College contribute to the endurance of its reputation. Once the discourse surrounding reputation gathers speed and spreads, it turns into a naturalized account of reality and constitutes social facticity "within a taken-for-granted system of norms, values, beliefs, and definitions" (Johnson, Dowd, & Ridgeway, 2006, p. 57). It "refers to the Real, but doesn't necessarily correspond with it" (Aronowitz, 2009, pp. 81-82). Reputation as "social fact" binds the institutional image to history and to social consciousness and soon becomes taken-for-granted knowledge. These "imagined" social facts (e.g. all students at McKinley College are ill-prepared and intellectually inferior, or working class students are more interested in and better suited to vocational education, and so on) endure over time. These notions endure despite challenges to the constructions of students from working-class backgrounds, as well as larger social, economic, and political shifts that ultimately permeate an institutional level, causing corresponding institutional shifts. However abstract, reputation acquires a certain durability over time, retains its value, and outlasts realities that exist outside of its construction.

The construction of reputation reveals a great deal about McKinley College and the larger field of higher education. Reputation is a powerful concept that is capable of simultaneously structuring institutional ethos and individual identities, or rather, institutional and individual habiti, and as such, deserves greater attention in scholarly research. Working-class reputation, as part of McKinley's institutional habitus, is also transmitted to and embodied by individuals within this particular organizational context through the differentiation of knowledge and discourse.

THE DIFFERENTIATION OF KNOWLEDGE AND DISCOURSE

With the growth and necessity of vocational majors, the discourse of higher education has shifted from one that was once liberal arts-centered (while often acknowledging the importance of and relationship to practical/applied forms of knowledge), to a dichotomous discourse in which a liberal arts education is discussed and imagined as separate from, and superior to, vocational education. This dichotomous discourse surrounding types of knowledge leads to two separate and classed discourses within higher education, reinforcing existing social demarcations. The proliferation of these competing discourses shape class-based distinctions, while clashing, dividing, and building a durable hierarchy of knowledge.

By way of example, the visual arts exist as a significant part of today's liberal arts education, but the visual arts, in particular, also have strong elitist roots and strongly contrasting anti-elitist rhetoric. This history cannot be ignored. Schools like McKinley, modeled after a traditionally elite liberal arts education, have arguably made it possible for students, formerly excluded from higher education's elite structure, to study the visual arts. This splintering has divided the inaccessible knowledge of the elite into the realm of the popular, and, as it continues to exist, within the realm of the elite. Economic and social demands have also splintered the practical knowledge, associated with the working classes, into the domain of the elite (increasing focus on professional and vocational knowledge within all institutions of higher education). Indeed, historical lines of separation that were once clearly drawn to indicate class distinctions are now seemingly blurred. This blurring however, contrary to dominant discourse, does not indicate a shift towards a more equal or level field of higher education, but in fact, seems to be quite the contrary.

This research, though focused on and within a "non-elite" space, tells us something about the relationship between what is elite and what is non-elite. "Elite" would mean very little if it did not exist among that which is considered "non-elite." The relationship itself offers unique insight into the structuring and potential restructuring of the field of higher education. Indeed, the concept of field itself is encapsulated by the relational mode of thinking (Bourdieu & Wacquant, 1992, xiii). Historically, and beginning with Harvard, the field of "higher" education was conceived at the outset as superior, elite, and exclusionary through its very language. At the same time, the "non-elite," relationally speaking, was a space constructed outside of higher education's still nebulous boundaries. Through democratization, however, positioning within the academic field expanded to include more accessible institutions and sub-fields, valuing different forms of academic capital, but these forms of capital, over time, held little value within the academic field. All the while, a durable hierarchy of class, knowledge, and capital was taking shape under the notion of increasing access. Democratization itself, rather than critically and reflexively examined, was (and still is) accepted as morally responsible and inherently sound.

THE RESIDUAL IMAGES OF DEMOCRATIZATION

The image of academic life at McKinley College, the "Harvard on the Lake," settles into a space carved out of the rhetoric of accessibility and democratization. If indeed an elitist, liberal arts education resists democratization, then democratization, despite its good intentions, becomes a false ideology, helping instead to perpetuate durable social inequalities. As such, images of McKinley College provoke questions about the artificiality of time-wrapped institutions—those that build upon, and are built upon, *residual images and reproductions* of an elite past that once comprised the field of higher education. Just as it has been contended in the visual arts since the "Age of Mechanical Reproduction," something is lost through the process of the reproduction of images: "One might argue that all reproductions more or less distort" (Berger, 1977, p. 20). In this way, distortion implies an object that has been stripped of its original, authentic qualities (or rather, its "aura" according to Benjamin, 1969), but this process does not necessarily mean that the reproduction itself is of a poorer quality. More importantly, reproductions appear to distort original meaning by creating multiple meanings through a multiplicity of uses and for a multiplying audience. For example, art prints (reproductions of original works of art) made "high art" accessible to a public otherwise excluded. But artworks, if truly reproduced for accessibility, do not merely exist within a circuit of inexhaustible mimicry, but are alive for interpretation and the production of new meanings and uses that lie outside of academic, art historical discourse; however, these new ways of seeing and interpreting the images of art history remain unrecognized, and worse, devalued as insignificant, uninformed notions if they fail to enter into the dominant structure and language of the academy. If reproductions do indeed distort, then the distortion seems to be an inherent characteristic of the process of democratization set off within a hegemonic social structure. As the (elite) knowledge of surrounding art is disseminated within a non-elite space (one that has been democratized), and is consumed by a non-elite audience, absorbed into a non-elite discourse, the meanings become silent voids among the more "disciplined" and "legitimate" discourses of the intellectual field, namely that of art history, theory, and criticism. Under this logic, and as a democratized, "working-class" institution, McKinley College appears as a deficient duplicate—as the residual images of a democratization filter, or rather, what remains of the elite original that has been altered through social process. However, like visual reproductions, McKinley College is lacking neither in value, intelligence, nor meaning, but perhaps lacking only in comparative position among the privileged position of "originals" within the field of higher education. It is the process of democratization, then, and the field of higher education itself that demand re-conception.[1]

RE-CONCEIVING THE LIMITED DISCOURSE AND DIRECTION OF DEMOCRATIZATION

Within this text, democratization has been expressed as a well-intended, socially responsible process aimed at reducing inequality by increasing access to the once exclusionary cultural and social capital of the elite (institutions of higher education, credentials, knowledge, and so forth) and thereby increasing equality of opportunity. McKinley College, as a liberal-arts-focused institution that admits a majority of students from working class backgrounds, offers opportunities for students to acquire a liberal arts education at a price that is comparatively affordable. But, if "cultural 'habits and dispositions' comprise a resource capable of generating 'profits'" (Weninger & Lareau, 2003), does the cost outweigh the value of more affordable higher education? Does admission to these more accessible schools offer equality of opportunity and the chance for real social mobility? In other words, is something indeed lost through the process of democratization?

As a social process, and as currently conceived, democratization is discriminatory and selective as it attempts to "democratize" only the exclusionary knowledge, institutions, and cultural capital of the elite; however, the reversal remains inconceivable. Democratization, as understood through public and academic discourse, neglects to recognize that all people, from all respective class backgrounds possess and accumulate cultural capital specific to individual and class habitus. Presented this way, democratization itself appears inherently flawed and unidirectional in its conception as it disregards and devalues the capital of the "non-elite" while reaffirming the capital of the elite. The very notion that the highly valued products and knowledge of the elite must be "democratized" for the non-elite is a reductionist notion that upholds and legitimizes the hierarchical structure of inequality—a very undemocratic notion indeed.

To begin re-examining, and ultimately re-conceiving democratization, we might turn the current conception on its head and ask why vocational education has yet to be "democratized" for the elite? We might then ask why more privileged students do not wish to study trades at institutions focusing on these kinds of offerings? And follow it up by asking why vocational education is not as highly valued (often de-valued) at more elite, prestigious institutions? Or, we might ask why vocational education is not as highly valued (again, often de-valued) by middle-class and upper-middle class families? One might be quick to offer a more individualistic answer to explain why someone from a more privileged background would not choose to become a mechanic—it is a simple lack of interest. Some might communicate the ridiculousness of the inquiry and disregard the seriousness of the question as it deviates from the acceptable, natural way of thinking. The real answer, of course, is because traditional "blue collar" jobs, the stuff of vocational education, are not as highly valued among the middle and upper classes. In fact, these jobs carry the weight of anti-intellectualism and social stigma. This is not unlike the question of interest and value of the visual arts that Bourdieu once tried to disentangle. In following Bourdieu's argument, we are not born to appreciate the arts, just as we are not born with a certain distaste or affinity for rebuilding a car engine.

However, even the initial act of calling the direction of democratization into question is problematic; the very notion of "access," a synonym for democratization in academic discourse (also used to describe this process are "open access," "equal educational opportunity," and "diversity"; Scott, 2006, p. 15) is also ill-conceived. When is access not used in reference to providing the lacking masses with "reproductions" of the capital of the elite ("the residual images of democratization")? Democratization exists as a vague kind of logic within the discursive realm of our moral and political interests; the process appeals to our sense of what is "right," but as it unfolds within the academic field without academic reflexivity, it spreads as an inchoate process, becomes stunted and unidirectional, and its consequences remain largely neglected and buried beneath good intentions.

Examining this notion further, the inherent failure of the social process of democratization, in addition to the ways in which it is valued outside of education by families of advantaged backgrounds, becomes the way in which it is conceived and structured by the field of higher education and academic discourse. The concept itself is caught up and trapped within mental and social structures that make up the academic field.

RE-CONCEIVING SOCIAL RESEARCH

Without reflexivity, this research would risk doubling back onto itself and re-eliting the very knowledge it seeks to question. Research that employs the language of the elite, from a privileged, hyper-competitive position within academia, easily finds itself sharing the same qualities of which it is critical. With reflexivity, however, this research meets the opportunity to resist the unconscious reproduction of the elite structure. Central to this discussion, democratization not only circulates within academic discourse (publications informing policy initiatives, etc.), but it was constructed by academic discourse and reflects the dominant values of the field of higher education (elite knowledge), while implicitly devaluing knowledge and capital that exist outside of its academic boundaries. Another dimension of this research is that it reveals the symbolic force and power of privilege through the deconstruction of a concept that is arguably central to its own survival: democratization. Democratization stands as evidence that academic discourse fails to consider that there are other fields and fields within those fields with various kinds of social, cultural, and symbolic capital, as well as different values afforded to those various species of capital. For example, within this research, bifurcation and hierarchy of knowledge are built into the very conception of democratization (that which is valued by the elite and elite institutions is to be valued more so than other forms of knowledge). In these ways, democratization becomes an instrument of power, through the neglect of reflexivity and relational thinking, to which I now turn.

RE-CONCEIVING THE DIRECTION OF SOCIAL RESEARCH

With recent growth in response to Nader's (1974) call to study up (Cookson & Persell, 1985; Gaztambide-Fernández, 2006, 2009; Howard, 2007, 2008; Khan, 2008; Proweller, 1998), our understanding of elite identity formation and elite contexts has contributed a great deal to our understanding of privilege, but to date, scholarship has ignored the path privilege takes in all contexts. In other words, none have sought to follow elite discourse and knowledge into less elite contexts as an alternative approach to studying up. I argue that part of the reason for this omission is due to our casual disregard for the power of how we too play a critical role in creating dualisms and categories that create antagonisms and distinguish hierarchies of value. To this end, studying "elite knowledge" within a "non-elite" context allows for, and insists upon, the re-articulation of studying up *and down*. In the context of McKinley College, the directional pull of up and down as a strict dichotomous conceptualization does not provide an adequate space for the nuance and complexity of contemporary higher education, nor does it provide adequate space for the kind of relational thinking promoted by Bourdieu. Bourdieu's notion of relational thinking works to organically fuse concepts that would otherwise be separate and distinct by focusing instead on their relationships. With a relational understanding of the social world, including its concepts (elite versus non elite) we break with an often involuntary (or unconscious) drawing of distinctions (like focusing solely on the elite, or rather, elite knowledge within elite space). In attempting to think outside of these binary oppositions, studying up is insufficient without at once studying down. Because this research is committed to the collapse of these conceptualizations, the study of elite knowledge within a non-elite space (as defined by its position within the field of higher education) has been highlighted as a theoretical/methodological contribution to the study of privilege and also as an elaboration of Bourdieu's theoretical framework. As McKinley and other democratized spaces make clear, studying up *or* down seem to be inappropriate terms for the study of social space. We must study up *and* down. Without a re-conception of terms, not just their re-articulation, our own academic discourse inhibits our ability to get under the surface to track and reveal the more hidden mechanisms involved in the differentiation of knowledge and social space. While democratization sits here on its head, it seems useful to continue from this renewed perspective and move toward a democratization that is capable of realizing its original goals. As we move forward, re-conceiving seems all the more important. As Donoghue (2008) predicts:

> Like American society as a whole, with its widening gap between haves and have-nots, America's universities will grow increasingly stratified. The elite, privileged universities and colleges (about 100 of them, according to Barron's and similar surveys) will continue to function much as they do today, championing the liberal arts and the humanities and educating the children of the elite and privileged sector, and, or course, their own exclusive brand of higher education. . . . The gulf between these elite universities and the institutions that educate everyone else will widen in new ways that will complicate our efforts to define both the idea of higher education and the concept of access to higher education. (p. 84)

TOWARDS DEMOCRATIZATION

Access to Inequality is not another reductive account of working-class lack. Instead, this book acknowledges that the consequences generated by democratization are cross-cutting groups and fields. This book bends our thinking back to understand that all classes and groups not only deserve equal opportunities, but the chance to develop interests and pathways that derive from real choice rather than "choice" that is based upon hierarchical class structure. But, as Bourdieu asserts: "To denounce hierarchy does not get us anywhere. What must be changed are the conditions that make this hierarchy exist, both in reality and in minds" (Bourdieu & Wacquant, 1992, p. 84). Appropriately then, this book ends with recommendations to urge us toward *somewhere*. To be clear, these recommendations go well beyond the classroom, as this is not an issue of individual students and teachers, but a struggle against the effects (and *affects*) produced through democratization.[2]

If democratization is to meet its goals, we (society) must break with common binary oppositions (hand versus head, blue versus white, vocational versus academic) that bind the working classes to harmful historical representations and to an inferior status and reputation in education. The real challenge of course becomes a matter of how to establish such a fundamental shift in consciousness and valuation of various forms of knowledge. This research suggests that such a shift should begin within the academy itself—the very space that all too often neglects its own troubled, exclusionary history, and the very space where this book, too, has the potential to function either as a tool for transformation or as a tool to reproduce symbolic violence. In more practical terms, this book urges scholars (the producers of new knowledge—elite knowledge) to recognize the capacity of scholarship to aid in the construction of socially harmful realities. Further, this book urges scholars, sociologists in particular, to practice deeper levels of reflexivity,[3] which requires a sociology of sociology itself, as well as relational understandings of the social world.

On a policy level, I join a relatively small group of scholars who suggest that higher education must cease its reliance upon expansion (Mullen, 2010; Reay, 2012). Though expansion has indeed created greater opportunities for lower-income and minority students, access has led to further inequality. The system cannot continue to expand and expect equality of opportunity or an overall leveling of equality (Mullen, 2010). Mullen, I believe, rightly asserts: "If previous trends give us any guidance for the future, expansion will only further entrench educational differentiation, whereby new distinctions (of either institutions or fields of study) will become even more prominent" (p. 221). However, this does not mean abandoning policies aimed at supporting underserved students, nor does it mean abandoning approaches designed to improve access to postsecondary education, particularly to elite institutions. Such policies are largely necessary and can be very effective, but marginally so (Mullen, 2010).

Finally, as democratization legitimates differentiation, and as a result, inequality, differentiation within and between institutions of higher education should be re-evaluated and revised. But, differentiation will always retain a hierarchical structure of knowledge until vocational knowledge is valued and revalorized. I agree with Diane Reay (2012) in suggesting a revalorizing of vocational knowledge. She writes:

> A revalorizing of vocational and working-class knowledge and a broadening out of what constitutes educational success beyond the narrowly academic are long overdue. But that requires far more than the reestablishment of separate vocational and academic tracks. It needs a revaluing and respect for what those in the working class have traditionally done alongside a recognition of their potential to do very different things, if provided with adequate support. (p. 3)

This kind of movement would require attention to vocational knowledge as a respected form of academic knowledge at all levels of education (K-12)—a significant shift from its current hierarchical location.

In the end, this research points not only to democratization as a force in structuring unequal social space, but to the construction of this term, or rather, to the mechanisms that maintain its hierarchical conditions. To cause a fissure in this unequal structure, fundamental changes in the ways in which we think and construct our own scholarship (to incorporate reflexivity and relational thinking, to recognize there is value in other fields, sub fields, and forms of capital) must first be realized. However, these kinds of fundamental breaks require collective shifts of consciousness and more than a sense of moral obligation, where real democratization currently sits and waits.

NOTES

1. Part of this section is based upon an article written by the author. The final, definitive version of this paper has been published in *Cultural Studies <=> Critical Methodologies*, Volume 11, Number 1, February/2011, by SAGE Publications Ltd./SAGE Publications, Inc., All rights reserved.

2. Current debates surrounding grade inflation, arguably a product of multiple forces and processes (democratization is but one), exemplify this argument.

3. By way of example, professors might question why teacher-training is such a neglected part of our own formal educational experiences? Is this neglect based upon antiquated, elitist thinking about the role of the university professor—thinking that suggests teaching is less important than producing new knowledge? Our scholarly priorities and positions are quite telling, I think.

Appendix

ON METHODOLOGY

The following overall question guided this qualitative research: To what extent does a public liberal arts institution (specifically, a four-year comprehensive state college and its associated art museum) re/produce and transmit "elite" knowledge, and how do students, faculty, administration, and museum staff articulate their experiences with, and their perceptions of, the visual arts as part of higher education?

In answering this question, semi-structured, open-ended interviews were conducted with fifteen students (five students enrolled in the art history program and ten students enrolled in various degree programs); four art historians/professors of art history; five full-time faculty members within departments outside of the arts; five members of the museum staff (from the total of thirteen full-time positions); and four college administrators (including the president)—a total of thirty-three interviews. To determine which students, faculty, and administration to interview, I used the snowball sampling technique (Bogdan & Biklen, 2003, p. 64). As I proceeded, however, sampling became slightly more purposeful—gathering students and faculty from a wide range of disciplines, or as I determined, gathering those who I believed I needed to interview (e.g. director of particular program). The snowball technique was deemed the most effective way to connect with students, faculty, and administration across a large college campus. Criteria then, were context-specific, but also depended upon finding students and faculty within a wide variety of disciplines and years of experience. For example, I knew at the outset of this research that I needed a sample that included diverse perspectives, and had I interviewed all first-year students, my data may be skewed by lack of experience—students' perspectives often change as they adapt to a new environment.

All participants were asked the same set of interview questions, loosely designed around demographic and substantive questions related to experiences working at or attending McKinley College or its affiliated art museum (MMA) and perceptions of these institutions (particular to their current positions and identities). These paths of inquiry were then followed by several questions regarding their perceptions of and involvement in the arts. Interviews were recorded in accordance with each participant's signed consent and later transcribed by an outside source. To secure the anonymity of all participants, individuals and institutions were assigned pseudonyms upon the transcription of interviews. To further conceal the identity of the participants, the school, the art museum, and the location of the institution within its respective city has been geographically expanded and loosely identified as one of many larger cities within the Northeast.

Non-participant observations, along with interviews and document analysis, allow for a deeper, more complex, and multidimensional analysis of the college and museum. Unlike participant observations wherein the researcher becomes a member of the group, non-participant observers "stand aloof from the group activities they are investigating and eschew group membership" (Cohen, Manion, & Morrison, 2007, p. 259). Though it is indeed difficult to resist membership or participation in a natural social environment, like that of a classroom (as opposed to a laboratory setting, for example), it was preferable in my situation to sit among students in the back of a classroom and blend in, particularly within a large lecture hall. In addition, I found passing as an undergraduate student relatively easy given my age and appearance at the time of data collection—I was still in my twenties and consciously chose clothing that would not call attention to my professional purpose (e.g., replacing my blazer for a hooded sweatshirt). Though hyper-aware of my position as an outsider, I never once noticed a look of confusion or a suspicious glance. I found it easy to enter the classroom with students and leave with the crowd. Following the consent of two professors within the art history program, I observed one higher-level class and two introductory classes during the 2008 fall semester. While an observer, I recorded written and typed (when appropriate) notes on my interpretations of student engagement and reception, pedagogic practice, and details relevant to the study ("classroom talk"). Classroom observations allowed for greater depth in analysis of the dissemination of "elite" knowledge.

During general campus observations (e.g. while waiting for interviewees, having lunch or coffee in the Student Union, or reflecting after interviews) I collected field notes detailing the visible surroundings (architecture, student interactions, and so forth) to contribute to a deeper and more comprehensive understanding of the contexts of the college and museum. Observation notes were taken on-site or post-interview to record significant moments/events that arose while on location. I also attended public events held at the college and museum to observe who attended these events, when these events occurred, and analyzed the various forms of knowledge promoted by these events. Some of these events included public lectures at the college and exhibitions at the McKinley Museum of Art.

The third method, document analysis, included carefully examining college and museum publications, electronic sources (website) and larger advertising materials such as billboards, newspaper/magazine ads, and news releases (e.g. where the advertising is located, the target audience). Public documents are the museum's and the college's methods and materials for communicating with their publics—analysis of such documents was an essential component, allowing for a deeper understanding of how both the museum and college promote themselves in a competitive market, and often indicating which parts of the public are targeted for communicative exchange. All documents collected are accessible to the public and were obtained electronically, or through visits to the museum and the college. Most documents (e.g. museum publications, course syllabi) are paper-based and were collected in their original forms. Web-based documents were printed into hard-copy form to ensure accuracy and completeness (Hatch, 2001, p. 123).

On visits to the McKinley Museum, I collected internally produced, museum publications (exhibition brochures and museum documents describing the building, programming, and the permanent collection), and gathered newspaper clippings (some original hard copy and others printed from web-based material) relevant to the Museum. In addition, after speaking with, and formally interviewing staff at the Museum, I was able to contact particular individuals for help in accessing internal visitor statistics and historical/archival documents (copied and provided by staff for my research purposes). Upon visits to McKinley College, I collected public departmental documents (particularly within the Fine Arts Department, of which art history is part), internally produced college publications (e.g., brochures, alumni newsletters, college newsletters, honors-specific newsletters, the general college website, with particular attention to the arts—all relevant sources were printed for analysis), and accessed college statistics via the Office of Institutional Research. Specific to this research on the differentiation of knowledge, course syllabi were particularly important to the collection of data on standards and expectations of McKinley Art History students. Syllabi were also accessed and printed from the web pages of other institutions to generate document-based comparisons of art history courses.

ESTABLISHING AND GAINING ACCESS

General access to students, faculty, and administration was obtained through an electronic message to the President of McKinley College, which detailed my research objectives, requested permission to conduct research within this institution, and also requested a personal interview. To my advantage, the President and I had mutual acquaintances and I also expressed my interest as a McKinley alumna. I then contacted the Director of the McKinley Museum of Art, requesting an interview as well as permission to interview staff. The director declined my request for a personal interview, as he was too busy with the building transition. This was disappointing, but understandable given the demands of such a project. I was, however, able to reach several staff members (via recommendations) who were willing to participate. One particular staff member was a former acquaintance who I had known from working at the International Museum of Art (the art museum located directly across the street from the McKinley Museum of Art). She initially declined after a phone conversation, indicating she was concerned about discussing the museum, as she was newly employed; however, with persistence I was able to convince her to interview after having met with several of her colleagues. Access was indeed always a concern, in the beginning, during, and nearing the end of my research. In fact, I was never granted full access to the Art History Program. After contacting the Chair of the department with a brief description of my research, he declined my request for an interview and for particular information regarding students (names of potential interviewees), without explanation. The reason for his dismissal remains entirely unclear, but speculation suggests that he, or other key people within a very small, perhaps vulnerable, department (in the process of going through restructuring, e.g. at the time of my research, a Professor of Philosophy was Interim Chair), were somehow threatened by my research topic. Perhaps the concept "elite knowledge" was perceived as a kind of attack on art history? Perhaps the value-laden word "elite" provoked an unintended response? Perhaps it is too close to "elitism" or "elitist"? In the end, I was able to connect with one retired art history professor who was more than willing to participate and offered recommendations for additional participants. Without the Chair's approval, I was limited to a very small sample of art history students and part-time or retired faculty (a program that is small to begin with). Data collection (observations and interviews) commenced in the summer of 2008, following several visits to the college and the art museum during the month of February through May of 2008.[1]

NOTE

1. The author would like to thank the Mark Diamond Foundation for the generous funding of the research informing this book.

References

Agger, B. (1989). Fast capitalism. Urbana: University of Illinois Press.

Alba, R.D. & Lavin, D.E. (1981). Community colleges and tracking in higher education. *Sociology of Education, 54*, 223-237.

Anyon, J. (1980). Social class and the hidden curriculum of work. *Journal of Education, 162*(1), 7-92.

Anyon, J. (1981). Social class and school knowledge. *Curriculum Inquiry, 11*(1), 3-42.

Aries, E. & Seider, M. (2005). The interactive relationship between class identity and the college experience: The case of lower income students. *Qualitative Sociology, 28*(4), 419-443.

Aronowitz, S. (2004). *How class works: Power and social movement*. New Haven, CT: Yale University Press.

Aronowitz, S. (2009). Facing the economic crisis. *Situations, 3*(1), 23-34.

Aronowitz, S. & Giroux, H. A. (1987). *Education under siege: The conservative, liberal and radical debate over schooling*. London: Routledge.

Arum, R., Gamoran, A., & Shavit, Y. (2007). *Stratification in higher education: A comparative study*. Stanford, CA: Stanford University Press.

Arum, R. & Shavit, Y. (1994). *Another look at tracking: Vocational education and social reproduction*. Florence: European University Institute.

Astin, A.W. (1993). What matters in college: Four critical years revisited. San Francisco, CA: Jossey-Bass.

Astin, A.W. & Oseguera, L. (2004). The declining equity of American higher education. The Review of Higher Education, 27(3), 321-341.

Bachelard, G. (1994). *The poetics of space*. Boston, MA: Beacon Press.

Bastedo, M.N. & Gumport, P.J. (2003). Access to what? Mission differentiation and academic stratification in US public higher education. *Higher Education, 46*, 341-359.

Baxter, A. & Brinton, C. (2001). Risk identity and change: Becoming a mature student. International Studies in the Sociology of Education, 11(1), 87-102.

Becker, H. (1982). *Art worlds*. Berkeley: University of California Press.

Benjamin, W. (1969). *Illuminations: Essays and reflections*. New York: Schocken Books.

Berger, J. (1990). *Ways of seeing*. UK: Penguin.

Berger, P.L. & Luckman, T. (2002).The social construction of reality [1996]. In C.J. Calhoun, J. Gerteis, J. Moody, S. Pfaff, & V. Indermohan (Eds.), *Contemporary sociological theory* (pp. 43-51). Malden, MA: Blackwell Publishing.

Bernstein, B. (1977). *Towards a theory of educational transmissions*. London: Routledge.

Boden, M.A. (2000). Craft, perception and the possibilities of the body. *British Journal of Aesthetics, 40*(3), 289-301.

References

Bogdan, R.C. & Biklen, S. (2003). *Qualitative research for education: An introduction to theory and methods.* Boston: Allyn & Bacon.

Bok, D. (2006). *Our underachieving colleges: A candid look at how much students learn and why they should be learning more.* Princeton and Oxford: Princeton University Press.

Bourdieu, P. (1977). *Outline of a theory of practice.* Cambridge: Cambridge University Press.

Bourdieu, P. (1984). *Distinction: A social critique of the judgment of taste.* Cambridge, MA: Harvard University Press.

Bourdieu, P. (1988). *Homo academicus.* Stanford, CA: Stanford University Press.

Bourdieu, P. (1989). *The state nobility: Elite schools in the field of power.* Stanford, CA: Stanford University Press.

Bourdieu, P. (1990). The Logic of Practice. Stanford, CA: Stanford University Press.

Bourdieu, P. (1991). *Language and symbolic power.* UK: Polity Press.

Bourdieu, P. (1993). *The field of cultural production.* New York: Columbia University Press.

Bourdieu, P. (1996). *The rules of art: Genesis and structure of the literary field.* Stanford, CA: Stanford University Press.

Bourdieu, P. (2008). *Sketch for a self-analysis.* Chicago and London: The University of Chicago Press.

Bourdieu, P. & Passeron, J.C. (2000). *Reproduction in education, society and culture.* London: Sage.

Bourdieu, P. & Wacquant, L.J.D. (1992). *An invitation to reflexive sociology.* Chicago: The University of Chicago Press.

Bowen, W.G. & Bok, D. (2000). *The shape of the river: Long-term consequences of considering race in college and university admissions.* Princeton: Princeton University Press.

Bowen, W.G., Chingos, M.M. & McPherson M.S. (2009). Crossing the finish line: Completing college at America's public universities. Princeton, NJ: Princeton University Press.

Brantlinger, E. (2003). *Dividing classes: How the middle class negotiates and rationalizes school advantage.* New York and London: RoutledgeFalmer.

Broido, E.M. (2004).Understanding diversity in millennial students. *New Directions for Student Services, 106,* 73-85.

Brooks, R.L. (2005). Measuring university quality. *The Review of Higher Education, 29*(1): 1-21.

Brown, P. & Hasketh, A. (2004). *The mismanagement of talent: Employability and jobs in the knowledge economy.* Oxford: Oxford University Press.

Brown, P. Lauder, H. & Ashton, D. (2011). The global auction: The promise of education, jobs, and income. New York: Oxford University Press USA.

Bryson, J.R., Daniels, P.W., Henry, N., & Pollard, J. (1997). *Knowledge, space, economy.* London: Routledge.

Burke, P.J. (2002). Toward a collaborative methodology: An ethnography of widening educational participation. *Australian Educational Researcher, 29*(1), 115-136.

Capriccioso, R. (January 26, 2006). Aiding first-generation students. *Inside Higher Education.* http://www.insidehighered.com/news/2006/01/26/freshmen

Charmaz, K. (2005). Grounded theory in the 21st century: Applications for advancing social justice studies. In N. Denzin and Y. Lincoln (Eds.), *The Sage Handbook of Qualitative Research,* (3rd ed. pp. 507-536). Thousand Oaks, CA: Sage Publications.

Chronicle of Higher Education. (January 21, 2010). This year's freshmen at 4-year colleges: Highlights of a survey. http://chronicle.com/article/This-Years-Freshmen-at-4-Year/63672/

Clark, R. & Ivanic, R. (1997). *The politics of writing.* New York: Routledge.

Cohen, L., Manion, L., & Morrison, K.R.B. (2007). *Research methods in education.* New York: Routledge.

Cohen, P. (February 24, 2009). In tough times, the humanities must justify their worth. *New York Times.* http://www.nytimes.com/2009/02/25/books/25human.html

Collins, J. (2002). *High Pop: Making culture into popular entertainment.* Malden, MA: Blackwell Publishers.

Cookson, P.W. & Persell, C.H. (1985). *Preparing for power: America's elite boarding schools.* New York: Basic Books.

Crichlow, W. (2003). Stan Douglas and the aesthetic critique of urban decline. In, G. Dimitriadis & D. Carlson (Eds.), *Promises to Keep: Cultural studies, democratic education and public life,* (pp. 155-166). New York: RoutledgeFalmer.

Cuno, J. (2004). *Whose muse?: Art museums and the public trust.* Princeton, NJ: Princeton University Press.

Danto, A. (1964). The artworld. The Journal of Philosophy, 61(19), 571-584.

Denzin, N. (1989). *Interpretive interactionism. Applied research methods series, 16.* Newbury Park, CA: Sage Publications.

Denzin, N. & Lincoln, Y. (2005). *The sage handbook of qualitative research* (3rd ed.). Thousand Oaks, CA: Sage Publications, Inc.

Dichev, I. (2001). News or noise? Estimating the noise in the U.S. news university rankings. *Research in Higher Education, 42,* 237-266.

DiMaggio, P. (1978). Social class and arts consumption: The origins and consequences of class differences in exposure to the arts in America. *Theory and Society, 5*(2), 141-161.

Donoghue, F. (2008). *The last of the professors: The corporate university and the fate of the humanities.* New York: Fordham University Press.

Dougherty, K.J. (1994). *The contradictory college: The conflicting origins, impacts and futures of the community college.* Albany, NY: State University of New York Press.

Duncan, C. (1993). Educating the rich. In: *The Aesthetics of Power: Essays in the critical history of art.* Cambridge: Cambridge University Press.

Durkheim, E. (1995: 1912). *The elementary forms of religious life.* New York: The Free Press.

Ebert-Schifferer, S. (2002). Art history and its audience. In C.W. Haxhausen (Ed.), *The two art histories: The museum and the university* (pp. 45-51). Williamstown, MA: Sterling and Francine Clark Art Institute.

Elkins, J. (2008). *Visual literacy.* New York: Routledge.

Ellwood, D., & Kane, T.J. (2000). Who is getting a college education: Family background and the growing gaps in enrollment. In S. Danziger and J. Waldfogel (Eds.), Securing the future (pp. 283-324). New York: Russell Sage Foundation

Emerson, R.M., Fretz, R.I. & Shaw, L.L. (1995). *Writing ethnographic fieldnotes.* Chicago: The University of Chicago Press.

Emler, N. (1990). A social psychology of reputation. *European Review of Social Psychology, 1*(1), 171-193.

Freie, C. & Bratt, K. (in press). Nice girls become teachers: Experiences of female first-generation college students majoring in elementary education. In, B. Porfilio and C.S. Malott (Eds.), *Critical constructions: Studies on education and society.* Charlotte, NC: Information Age Publishing.

Frey, N. & Fisher, D. (2008). *Teaching visual literacy: Using comic books, graphic novels, anime, cartoons, and more to develop comprehension and thinking skills.* Thousand Oaks, CA: Corwin Press.

Gamoran, A. (2001). American schooling and educational inequality: A forecast for the 21st century. *Sociology of Education, Extra Issue,* 135-153.

Gamoran, A. (2008). Persisting social class inequality in U.S. education. In L. Weis (Ed.), *The way class works: Readings on school, family, and the economy* (pp. 169-179). New York and London: Routledge.

Gartman, D. (1991). Culture as class symbolization or mass reification? A critique of bourdieu's distinction. *The American Journal of Sociology, 97*(2), 421-447.

Gaztambide-Fernández, R. (2006). Lives of distinction: Ideology, space, and ritual in processes of identification at an elite boarding school. Unpublished Dissertation. Harvard University.

Gaztambide-Fernández, R. (2009). *The best of the best: Becoming elite at an American boarding school.* Cambridge and London: Harvard University Press.

Gee, J.P. (2005). *An introduction to discourse analysis: Theory and method.* London: Routledge.

Gee, J. (2006). Self-fashioning and shape-shifting: Language, identity and social class. In: D.E. Alverman, K.A. Hinchman, D.W. Moore, S.F. Phelps, & D.R. Waff (Eds.), *Reconceptualizing the literacies in adolescents' lives.* Mahway, NJ: Lawrence Erlbaum Associates, Inc.

Goyette, K.A. & Mullen, A. (2006). Who studies the arts and sciences? Social background and the choice and consequences of undergraduate field of study. *The Journal of Higher Education, 77*(3), 497-538.

Grenfell, M. & James, D. (1998). Bourdieu and education: Acts of practical theory. London: Falmer Pres.

Gutierrez, K.D. (1995). Unpacking academic discourse. *Discourse Processes, 19*, 21-37.

Hanks, W.F. (2005). Pierre Bourdieu and the practices of language. *Annual Review of Anthropology, 34*, 67-83.

Harris, J. (2001). *The new art history: A critical introduction*. London: Routledge.

Harrison, J., MacGibbon, L., & Morton, M. (2001). Regimes of trustworthiness in qualitative research: The rigors of reciprocity. *Qualitative Inquiry, 7*(3), 323-345. http://www.gsas.harvard.edu/programs_of_study/history_of_art_and_architecture.php

Harvey, (2005). *A brief history of neoliberalism*. New York: Oxford University Press.

Hatch, J.A. (2002). *Doing qualitative research in educational settings*. Albany, NY: State University of New York Press.

Haxthausen, C.W. (1999). *The two art histories: The museum and the university*. Williamstown, MA: Sterling and Francis Clark Art Institute.

Hofstadter, R. (1963). *Anti-intellectualism in American life*. New York: Knopf.

Hoglund, K.G. (1984). The museum trail: The collections at Yale university. *The Biblical Archaeologist, 47*(3), 160-165.

Hollingsworth, S. & Archer, L. (2009). Urban schools as urban places: School reputation, children's identities and engagement with education in London. *Urban Studies, 47*(3), 584-603.

hooks, b. (2000). *Where we stand: Class matters*. New York: Routledge.

Horvat, E.M.N. & Antonio, A.L. (1999). "Hey, those shoes are out of uniform': African American girls in an elite high school and the importance of habitus. *Anthropology & Education Quarterly, 30*(3), 317-342.

Howard, A. (2008). *Learning privilege: Lessons of power and identity in affluent schooling*. New York: Routledge.

Ivanic, R. (2004). Intertextual practices in the construction of multimodal texts in inquiry-based learning. In N. Shuart-Faris & D. Bloome (Eds.), *Uses of intertextuality in classroom and educational research*. (pp. 317- 352). Charlotte, NC: Information Age Publishing.

Jencks, C. & Riesman, D. (1968). *The academic revolution*. Chicago: University of Chicago Press.

Johnson, C., Dowd, T.J., & Ridgeway, C.L. (2006). Legitimacy as a social process. *Annual Review of Sociology, 32*, 53-78.

Karen, D. (2002). Changes in access to higher education in the United States: 1980-1992. *Sociology of Education, 75*, 191-210.

Katz, P.M. (2010). Service despite stress: Museum attendance and funding in a year of recession. A Report from the American Association of Museums.

Keller, B. (2005). *Class matters*. New York: New York Times Company.

Kerchoff, A.C. (2001). Education and social stratification processes in comparative perspective. *Sociology of Education, 74*(Special Issue), 3-18.

Khan, S.R. (2008). The production of privilege. Unpublished Dissertation. University of Wisconsin-Madison.

Kleiner, F.S. (2009). *Gardner's art through the ages: The western perspective*. Boston, MA: Wadsworth.

Lareau, A. & Conley, D. (2008). *Social class: How does it work?* New York: Russell Sage Foundation.

Leathwood, C. & O'Connel, P. (2003). 'It's a struggle': The construction of the 'new student' in higher education. Journal of Education Policy, 18(6), 597-615.

Lehman, W. (2009). University as vocational education: Working-class students' expectations for university. *British Journal of Sociology of Education, 30*(2), 137-149.

Lewis, H.R. (2006). *Excellence without a soul: How a great university forgot education*. New York: Public Affairs.

Lucas, S. (1999). *Tracking inequality: Stratification and mobility in American high schools.* New York: Teachers College Press.

McDonough, P. (1997). *Choosing colleges: How social class and schools structure opportunity.* New York: State University of New York Press.

McDonough, P. & Fann, A. (2007). The study of inequality. In P. Gumport (Ed.), *Sociology of Higher Education* (pp. 53-93). Baltimore: Johns Hopkins University Press.

Mills, C. (2008). Reproduction and transformation of inequalities in schooling: The transformative potential of the theoretical constructs of Bourdieu. *British Journal of Sociology of Education, 29*(1): 79-89.

Mills, C. & Gale, T. (2007). Researching social inequalities in education: Towards a bourdieuan methodology. *International Journal of Qualitative Studies in Education, 20*(4), 433-447.

Mitchell, K.D. (2008). *Finding their way: Cultural capital facilitators and first generation community college students.* Saarbrucken, Germany: VDM.

Morley, L. & Ansley, S. (2007). Employers, quality and standards in higher education: Shared values and vocabularies or elitism and inequalities? *Higher Education Quarterly, 61*(3), 229-249.

Morphew, C.C. & Hartley, M. (2006). Mission statements: A thematic analysis of rhetoric across institutional type. *Journal of Higher Education, 77*(3), 456-471.

Morphew, C.C. & Huisman, J.A. (2002). Using institutional theory to reframe research on academic drift. *Higher Education in Europe, 26*(4), 497-501.

Mullen, A.L. (2009). Elite destinations: Pathways to attending an ivy league. *British Journal of Sociology of Education, 30*(1), 15-27.

Mullen, A.L. (2010). *Degrees of inequality: Culture, class, and gender in American higher education.* Baltimore: The Johns Hopkins University Press.

Murdock, S.H. & Hoque, M. (1999). Demographic factors affecting higher education in the United States in the twenty-first century. *New Directions for Higher Education, 108*, 5-13.

Murray, C. (2003). Key writers on art: The twentieth century. London: Routledge.

Nader, L. (1974). Up the anthropologist: Perspectives gained from studying up. In Reinventing anthropology. In D.H. Hymes (Ed.), *Reinventing Anthropology,* (pp. 284-311). New York: Vintage Books.

Naidoo, R. (2004). Fields and institutional strategy: Bourdieu on the relationship between higher education, inequality and society. *British Journal of Sociology of Education, 25*(4): 457-471.

National Center Education Statistics. (2007-2008) Financial Aid Statistics. http://nces.ed.gov/fastfacts/display.asp?id=31

Oakes, J. (1985). Keeping track: How schools structure inequality. New Haven, CT: Yale University Press.

Oakes, J. (2005). *Keeping track: How schools structure inequality.* New Haven, CT: Yale University Press.

Oakes, J. (2008). *Beyond tracking: Multiple pathways to college, career, and civic participation.* Cambridge, MA: Harvard Education Press.

Piketty, R. & Saez, E. (2001). Income inequality in the United States, 1913-1998. (Working Paper 8467). Cambridge, MA: National Bureau of Economic Research.

Plattner, S. (1996). *High art down home: An economic ethnography of a local art market.* Chicago and London: The University of Chicago Press.

Powell, A.G. (2003). *Lessons from privilege: The American prep school tradition.* Cambridge, MA: Harvard University Press.

Proweller, A. (1998). *Constructing female identities: Meaning making in an upper middle class youth culture.* Albany, NY: State University of New York Press.

Reay, D. (1997). The double-bind of the "working class" feminist academic: The success of failure or the failure of success? In P. Mahony & C. Zmroczek (Eds.), *"Working-Class" Women's Perspectives on Social Class.* (pp. 18-29) London: Taylor & Francis.

Reay, D. (1998). Rethinking social class: Qualitative perspectives on gender and social class. *Sociology, 32*(2), 259-275.

Reay, D. (2001). Finding or losing yourself?: Working-class relationships to education. *Journal of Education Policy, 16*(4), 333-346.

Reay, D. (2003). A risky business?: Mature working class women students and access to higher education. *Gender and Education, 15*(3), 301-318.

Reay, D. (2004). It's all becoming a habitus: Beyond the habitual use of Pierre Bourdieu's concept of habitus in educational research. *British Journal of Sociology of Education, 25*(4), 431-444.

Reay, D. (2008). Class out of place: The white middle classes and intersectionalities of class and 'race' in urban state schooling in England. In L. Weis (Ed.), *The Way Class Works: Readings on School, Family, and the Economy*. New York: Routledge.

Reay, D. (2012). Schooling for democracy: A common school and common university? A response to 'schooling in democracy.' Democracy & Education, 19(1), 1-4.

Reay, D., Crozier, G., & Clayton, J. (2009). "Strangers in paradise?" Working-class students in elite universities. *Sociology, 43*(6), 1103-1121.

Reay, D. Crozier, G. & Clayton, J. (2010). 'Fitting in' or 'standing out': Working-class students in UK higher education. British Educational Research Journal, 32(1), 1-19.

Reay, D., David, M., & Ball, S. (2005). Degrees of choice: Social class, race, gender and higher education. London: Trentham Books Limited.

Reich, R. (2007). *Supercapitalism: The transformation of business, democracy, and everyday life*. New York: Alfred A. Knopf.

Reich, R. (2008). Why the rich are getting richer and the poor, poorer. In L. Weis (Ed.), *The way class works: Readings on school, family, and the economy* (pp. 13-24). New York: Routledge.

Rodden, J. (March/April, 2006). Reputation and its vicissitudes. *Culture and Society*, 75-80.

Roksa, J., Grodsky, E., Arum, R., & Gamoran, A. (2007). United States: Changes in higher education and social stratification. In Y. Shavit, R. Arum, & A. Gamoran (Eds.) *Stratification in Higher Education: A Comparative Study*, (pp. 165-194). Palo Alto: Stanford University Press.

Rose, M. (2004). The mind at work: Valuing the intelligence of the American worker. New York: Viking.

Scott, J.C. (2006). The mission of the university: Medieval to postmodern transformations. *Journal of Higher Education, 77*(1), 1-39.

Seidman, I. (2006*). Interviewing as qualitative research: A guide for researchers in education and the social sciences*. New York and London: Teachers College Press.

Shavit, Y., Arum, R. & Gamoran, A. (2007). *Stratification in higher education: A comparative study.* Stanford, CA: Stanford University Press.

Shofer, E. & Meyer, J.W. (2005). The worldwide expansion of higher education in the twentieth century. *American Sociological Review, 70*, 898-920.

Skeggs, B. (1997). Formations of class and gender. London: SAGE.

Soares, J.A. (2007). *The power of privilege: Yale and America's elite colleges.* Stanford, CA: Stanford University Press.

Stake, R.E. (2005). Qualitative case studies. In N. Denzin & Y. Lincoln (Eds.), *The Sage Handbook of Qualitative Research* (3rd ed., pp. 443-466). Thousand Oaks, CA: Sage Publications, Inc.

Stephan, J., Rosenbaum. J, & Person, A. (2009). Stratification in college entry and completion. Social Science Research, 38(3), 572-593.

Stevens, M. (2007). *Creating a class: College admissions and the education of elites.* Cambridge, MA: Harvard University Press.

Stewart, K. (2007). Ordinary Affects. Durham, NC: Duke University Press.

Stokstad, M. (2004). *Art history.* Upper Saddle River, NJ: Pearson Education, Inc.

Strathdee, R. (2009). Reputation in the sociology of education. *British Journal of Sociology of Education, 30*(1): 83-96.

Strauss, A.L. & Corbin, J. (1987). *Qualitative analysis for social scientists.* Cambridge, England: Cambridge University Press.

Swartz, D. (1997). *Culture and power: The sociology of pierre bourdieu.* Chicago, IL: The University of Chicago Press.

Thomas, S.L. & Bell, A. (2008). Education and class: Uneven patterns of opportunity and access. In L. Weis (Ed.), *The way class works: Readings on school, family and the economy.* New York: Routledge.

Thomas, S.L., & Perna, L.W. (2004). The opportunity agenda: A reexamination of postsecondary reward and opportunity. In J. Smart (Ed.), *Higher education: Handbook of theory and research, 19,* (pp.43-84). Dordrecht: Kluwer Press.

Tokarczyk, M. (2004). Promises to keep: Working class students and higher education. In M. Zweig (Ed.), What's class got to do with it? American Society in the Twenty First Century. (pp. 161-167). Ithaca, NY: Cornell University Press.

Trow, M.A. (2006). Reflections on the transition from elite to mass to universal access: Forms and phases of higher education in modern societies since WWII. In J.J.F. Forest & P.G. Altbach (Eds.), *International handbook of education,* (vol. 1 pp. 243-280). New York: Springer.

Tucker, A. (2002). Visual literacy: Writing about art. New York: McGraw-Hill

U.S. News & World Report (2009). Best Colleges 2010. http://colleges.usnews.rankingsandreviews.com/best-colleges

Wacquant, L. (2005). Carnal connections: On embodiment, apprenticeship, and membership. *Qualitative Sociology, 28*(4), 445-474.

Wallach, A. (2002). Class rites in the age of the blockbuster. In J. Collins, (Ed.) *High pop: Making culture into popular entertainment.* (pp. 114-128) Malden, MA: Blackwell Publishers.

Weis, L. (1990). *Working class without work. High school students in a de-industrializing economy.* New York: Routledge.

Weis, L. (2004). *Class reunion: The remaking of the American white working class.* New York: Routledge.

Weis, L. (2008). *The way class works: Readings on school, family, and the economy.* New York: Routledge.

Weis, L. (2011). Secondary education as a vehicle for achieving racial justice: A cautionary note based on the changing landscape of postsecondary education. Paper prepared for the *Ford Foundation Secondary Education and Racial Justice Collaborative, 1-36.*

Weis, L., McCarthy, C., & Dimitriadis, G. (2006). *Ideology, curriculum, and the new sociology of education.* New York: Routledge.

Weninger, E.B. & Lareau, A. (2003). Translating Bourdieu into the American context: The question of social class and family-school relations. *Poetics, 31,* 375-402.

Whitty, G. (2001). Education, social class and social exclusion. *Journal of Education Policy, 16*(4), 287-295.

Willis, P. (1977). *Learning to labor.* Farnborough, UK: Saxon House.

Zweig, M. (2000). *The working class majority.* Ithaca, NY: Cornell University Press.

Zweig, M. (2004). *What's class got to do with it?* Ithaca, NY: Cornell University Press.

Index

academic capital, 4, 11, 16, 19, 56, 59, 60, 66, 67, 72, 73, 78, 83, 105, 108; at McKinley, 11, 42, 71, 72, 76, 81

access: to art museums, 18–19, 23, 96, 97, 101; to higher education, 6, 7, 8, 62, 106, 109, 110, 111, 113, 114; to knowledge, 4, 5, 15, 63, 67n6, 75, 83, 108, 109. *See also* democratization

art museums, 13, 26, 74, 95, 97, 102; and colleges/universities, 9, 18, 19, 70, 71, 82, 94; history of, 17, 18, 70, 71, 95, 96, 97, 102; and McKinley students, 74, 99, 100

art history, 9, 16, 18, 70, 82, 83, 81, 94, 109; at McKinley, 11, 23, 35, 39, 41, 42, 47n5, 65, 66, 71, 82, 85, 86, 87, 87–88, 89, 90, 91, 92, 93, 94, 103n1

arts. *See* visual arts; liberal arts education

Bourdieu, Pierre, x, 3, 4, 10, 12n8, 14–23, 27n2, 29, 30, 32, 34, 59, 69, 70, 72, 97, 101, 105, 108, 111, 112, 113

class ceiling, 41, 58

college: and choice, 15, 34; and choice of major, 54; community colleges, 5, 8, 24, 37, 63, 64, 69, 70; as credential dispensing institution, 37, 38, 39, 42, 45; and differentiation, 51, 53; enrollment, 6, 7, 8, 34, 63; and equality, 2, 5; liberal arts colleges, 17, 52, 58, 72, 81, 85, 90, 110; mission statements, 60, 61, 62; and opportunity, 1, 2; rankings, 8, 11n2, 12n3, 43, 44, 55, 107; selectivity, 2, 3, 11n2, 12n3, 7, 24, 25, 39; state colleges, 25; and tier structure, 2, 3, 4, 7, 7–8, 11n2, 12n3, 24, 45, 52, 53, 62. *See also* higher education

cultural capital, 7, 14, 16, 19, 32, 34, 54, 59

curriculum, 32, 46; elementary and secondary, 52, 72, 73; at McKinley, 54, 77, 81; and tracking, 63. *See also* liberal arts education; vocational education

Democratization, 105, 108, 109, 110, 111, 112, 113, 114; of the arts, 9, 16, 70, 82, 96, 97; of elite knowledge, 4, 8, 9, 18, 19, 59, 96, 110, 111, 112, 114; of higher education, 6, 7, 9, 16, 25, 32, 52, 62, 106, 108, 114; and McKinley, 4, 39, 109

differentiation: institutional, 8, 51, 52, 59, 59–62, 114; of knowledge, 8, 11, 23, 50, 51, 52, 54, 59–62, 63, 66, 82, 90, 90–92, 107, 112, 113

discourse, 24, 32, 39, 42, 43, 46, 47n4; and the arts, 16, 17, 18, 19, 23, 71, 72, 73, 74, 75, 77, 78, 83, 84, 87, 90–102, 109; and higher education, 3, 4, 16, 17, 18, 19, 24, 32, 37, 38, 40, 42, 43, 45, 50, 52, 55, 58, 67n2, 70, 78, 82, 84, 107, 108, 110, 111, 112, 113; and

131

knowledge, 5, 6, 16, 18, 50, 51, 52, 53, 56, 59, 72, 112; and social class, 33, 38, 39, 40, 42, 50, 51, 52, 55, 73, 107

Duncan, Carol, 8, 9, 17, 25, 84, 91, 102, 106

Faculty, 6, 51, 62, 64; at McKinley, 10, 30, 33, 38, 40, 57, 61, 62, 64–65, 71, 77, 84, 94, 97; and students, 34, 36, 40, 41, 42, 43, 56, 107, 65, 72, 76, 77, 80, 81, 87, 98, 100, 100

field, 3, 4, 14, 15, 16, 22, 30, 32, 66, 69, 90, 92, 101, 102, 106, 109, 112, 113, 115; of the art world, 4, 9, 10, 11, 13, 16, 18, 19, 83, 97; of higher education (academic field, intellectual field), 3, 4, 9, 10, 13, 15, 16, 18, 19, 32, 34, 36, 45, 67, 70, 76, 78, 81, 83, 90, 94, 107, 108, 110, 112; homologous, 10, 16, 70, 94, 97

first generation students, 25, 26, 33, 37, 47n2, 54, 59

globalization, 4, 5, 6

habitus, 10, 11, 14, 15, 16, 32, 39, 66, 67, 71, 72, 76, 78, 80, 81, 107, 110; institutional, 15–16, 23, 32, 35–36, 67, 71, 78, 82, 84–85, 101, 102, 107; and intertextual habituality, 69, 72

Harvard University, 1, 2, 3, 8, 61, 62, 82, 94, 106, 108, 109

Higher Education, 2, 4, 5, 9, 13, 60; access to, 5, 6, 7, 8, 12n3, 18, 51, 62, 63, 113; and democratization, 5, 6, 8, 9, 16, 18–19, 37, 59, 62, 106, 109, 111–112, 114; expansion of, 5, 6–7, 51, 52, 53, 114; and policy, 114; and social class, 10, 11, 15, 16, 29–31, 33, 34, 37, 38, 40, 41, 42, 44, 54, 55, 56, 58, 81, 92, 107, 108, 111–112, 113; and stratification, 2, 3, 8, 14, 32, 39, 45, 52, 62, 64, 108; and the visual arts, 16, 17–18, 19, 70, 72, 76, 78, 79, 82, 83, 84, 87, 90, 94, 97, 109–110

honors programs, 64; at McKinley, 35, 57, 64, 65, 66, 84, 85, 93, 94

inequality, 2, 6, 7, 13, 18, 29, 45, 46, 52, 53, 82, 93, 105–106, 110, 114

knowledge: and the arts, 19, 25, 70–71, 75–76, 83–84, 93; bifurcated, 19, 49, 50, 51–54, 56, 58, 59, 66, 67n2, 78–82, 108; as capital, 4, 11, 14, 16, 19, 23, 32, 37, 42, 56, 59, 60, 66, 71, 72, 73, 76, 78, 81, 83, 101, 108, 111, 112, 115; differentiated, 8, 46, 49, 52, 59, 62, 66, 82, 107–109; democratized, 8, 17, 18, 110; and economy, 5–6; elite, 3, 4, 5, 8–9, 10, 13–14, 16, 17, 18–19, 25, 46, 61, 63, 67n6, 69, 70, 71, 71–72, 74, 79, 82, 83–84, 88, 90, 91, 93, 96, 102, 108, 109, 110, 111–113, 114; hierarchy, 6, 7, 8, 11, 13, 49–50, 70, 102, 108, 108–109, 114; at McKinley, 25, 50, 58, 59–60, 62, 64–66, 80, 84, 92, 99; and occupation, 45–46, 59–60; and tracking, 62–66. *See also* liberal arts education; vocational education; curriculum

legitimation, 43, 45, 46

liberal arts education: colleges, 10, 17, 51, 61, 62, 67n5, 84; content, 53, 57, 70; in decline, 53, 54; education, 8, 9, 16, 19, 38, 50, 52, 106, 109, 113; at McKinley College, 38, 42, 54, 55, 56, 57, 58, 59, 64, 73, 85, 110; and privilege, 53, 54, 55, 56, 59, 61, 72, 84, 113; and teaching, 90; and vocational education, 50, 51, 52, 53, 66, 108

literacy, 69, 71, 72; visual, 71–72, 76, 78, 79, 80, 91, 92, 93, 102, 103n1

meritocracy, 2, 39

ordinary affects, 30

postsecondary. *See* higher education

relational thinking, 2, 4, 10, 11, 14, 15, 16, 24, 35, 46, 66, 71, 73, 83, 108, 111, 112, 114, 115

reputation, 31, 32, 43, 44–45, 105, 107; and class, 9, 10, 11, 25, 29–30, 32, 40, 44, 50, 56, 78, 81, 90, 107, 114;

individual, 31; institutional, 2, 3, 9, 10, 11, 11n2, 25, 30, 31, 32, 32–33, 33–34, 36, 37, 39, 39, 40, 43, 44, 44–46, 50, 51, 52–53, 54, 56, 78, 81, 90, 107

Rust Belt, 2, 19, 20, 31

social class, 105; and choice of major, 54; and college choice, 15–16, 35, 37, 45, 113; and discourse, 51, 52, 56, 78, 81, 102, 108; and economy, 5, 105, 106; and elite knowledge, 19, 108; and geography, 13, 20–23, 24; and habitus, 15–16, 23, 35, 39, 67, 72, 76, 78, 85, 110; and higher education, 7, 23, 25, 29, 30, 34, 35, 40, 41, 44, 45, 54, 87, 105, 92, 106; and liberal arts education, 8, 9, 10, 16, 17, 19, 50, 51, 52, 54, 55, 56, 58, 59, 61, 62, 64, 66, 67n5, 70, 72, 84, 90, 106, 108, 109, 110, 113; and McKinley College, 10, 11, 25, 26, 33, 34, 37, 38, 39, 44, 45, 77, 102; middle class, 5, 6, 8, 25, 29, 34, 35, 36, 45, 46, 66, 77, 81, 111; and occupation, 49, 50, 60; and race, 6, 20, 55, 67n4; and reproduction, 4, 11, 13, 14, 19, 30, 32, 45, 50, 63, 67n3, 92, 102, 109, 112; and tracking, 62–64; upper class, 18, 111; and vocational education, 43, 50, 51, 52, 56, 58, 63, 66, 88, 107, 108, 110, 111; working class, 5, 9, 10, 11, 25–26, 29, 31, 33, 34, 35, 37, 38, 39, 40, 42,

43, 44, 45, 46, 49, 50, 52, 54, 55, 60, 66, 71, 77, 78, 79, 81, 87, 95, 102, 107, 108, 109, 110, 113, 114

students: and access to higher education, 2, 5, 6, 7, 8, 12n3, 15, 16, 18, 51, 52, 63, 108, 114; and choice of major, 54; and college choice, 15, 34, 56; and diversity, 6, 51; elite, 17, 90, 52, 94; and enrollment, 7, 24, 25, 45, 51; honors, 64–66, 93; at McKinley, 1, 11, 25, 26, 33, 34, 35, 36, 37, 38, 39, 40, 41, 42, 43, 44, 45, 55, 56, 57, 58, 59, 60, 62, 66, 71, 74, 78, 80, 81, 85, 88, 89, 90, 91, 93, 94, 99, 107; middle class, 34, 35, 36, 45; parent occupation/ background, 35; and race, 25, 55; working class, 10, 11, 29, 30, 34, 35, 39, 40, 43, 44, 45, 54, 56, 67, 78, 81, 87, 90, 102, 110. *See also* first generation students; visual arts and students

visual arts, 9, 11, 19, 70, 71, 73, 82, 108, 109, 111; at McKinley, 25, 26, 54, 67, 70, 71, 72, 74, 75, 78, 79, 80, 81, 82, 84, 94, 95, 97, 98, 100, 101, 102, 110; and students, 11, 17, 19, 23, 33, 71, 72, 73, 74, 75, 76, 77, 78, 79, 80, 81, 82, 83, 84, 85, 86, 90, 94, 97, 99, 100

vocational education, 5, 12n5, 43, 50, 51, 52, 56, 58, 63, 66, 67n1, 88, 107, 108, 110, 111, 114, 115

About the Author

Amy Elizabeth Stich received her PhD in sociology of education at the University at Buffalo, State University of New York, where she is currently a postdoctoral research associate. Her work focuses on issues of social class and inequality of opportunity in higher education. This is her first book.